Meiner Gisi
das Beste
& Horst
liebe Grüße
Euer Fritz
Kap 10

Dirk Meinzer

SIRENENHEIME
SIREN HOMES

*Texte von / Essays by
Annett Reckert, Andrea Tippel
& Tilmann Haffke*

Kunsthalle Göppingen

Ausstellung Kunsthalle Göppingen / Exhibition	7
Saturnoptikum / Saturnopticon	33
Sturmwinddämonen / Windstorm Demons	39
Bioaktive Subjekte / Bioactive Subjects	55
Lächler / Smilers	79
Präapokalyptikum / Preapocalypticon	109
rascha-rascha / rascha-rascha	115
Kleine Wolke / Little Cloud	127
Schreckpopanze / Scarecrows	133
Sirenenheime / Siren Homes	155
Transgression Exzess / Transgression Excess	167
Andere / Others	195
Texte / Texts	205
Anhang / Appendix	245

AUSSTELLUNG KUNSTHALLE GÖPPINGEN
EXHIBITION

SATURNOPTIKUM
SATURNOPTICON

1. *Saturnoptikum*, 2003–2009
Transparentspiegelfolie, Holz, Metall
Two-way mirror film, wood, metal
380 × 120 × 240 cm

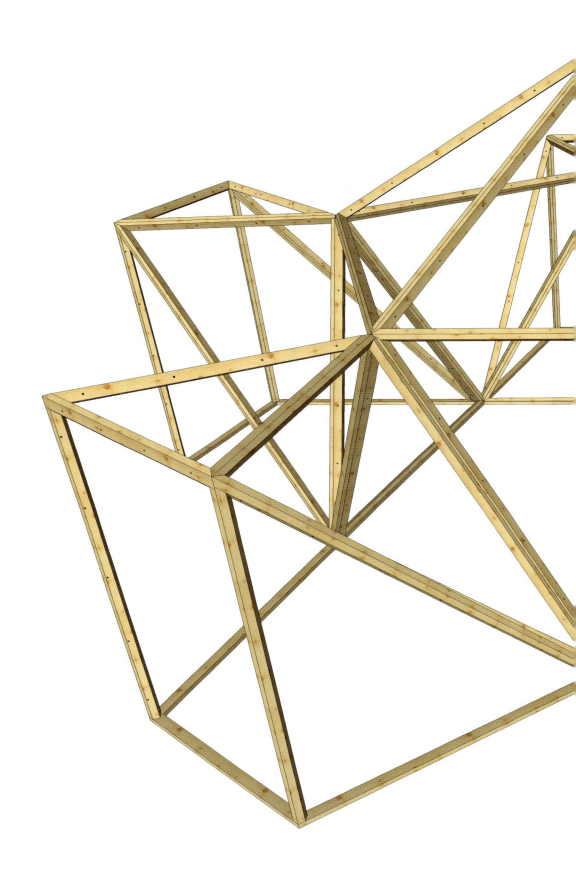

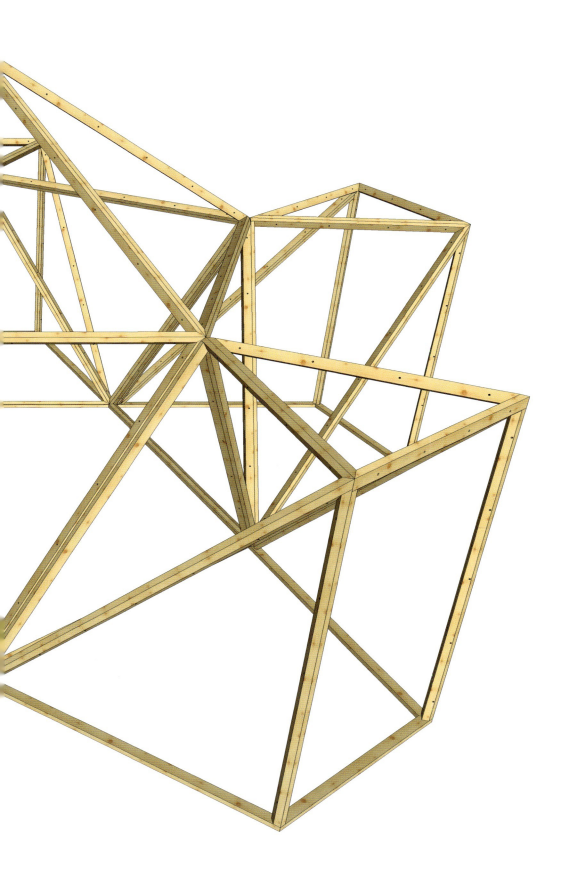

STURMWINDDÄMONEN
WINDSTORM DEMONS

2. *Kumbi-Kumbi Sturmwinddämon,* 2004
Insektenflügel, Leim, Lack auf Pappe
Insect wings, glue, lacquer on paper
24 × 18 cm

3. *Sturmwinddämon Himmel*, 2005
Insektenflügel, Leim, Lack auf Pappe
Insect wings, glue, lacquer on paper
23 × 17 cm

4. *Sturmwinddämon I*, 2004
Insektenflügel, Leim
Insect wings, glue
19,5 × 15 cm

5. *upepo V*, 2006
Insektenflügel, Leim
Insect wings, glue
15 × 10 cm

6. *Sturmwinddämon III*, 2004
Insektenflügel, Leim
Insect wings, glue
15,5 × 20 cm

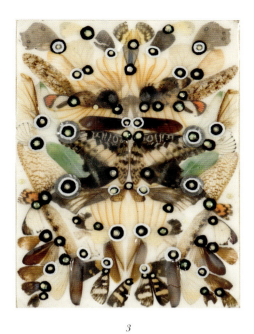

3

4

6

5

7. *Sturmwinddämon II,* 2004
Insektenflügel, Leim
Insect wings, glue
12,5 × 10 cm

Folgende Doppelseite / Next spread

8. *kleiner Sturmwinddämon,* 2004
Insektenflügel, Leim, Lack auf Pappe
Insect wings, glue, lacquer on paper
11 × 9 cm

9. *dunkler Sturmwinddämon,* 2004
Insektenflügel, Leim, Lack auf Pappe
Insect wings, glue, lacquer on paper
18 × 15 cm

7

8

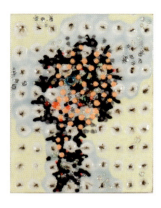

10

11

10. *upepo I*, 2005
Fluoreszentes, Mücken auf Papier
Fluorescent paint, midges on paper
14 × 11 cm

11. *upepo II*, 2005
Fluoreszentes, Mücken auf Papier
Fluorescent paint, midges on paper
14,5 × 10 cm

12. *upepo IV*, 2006
Fluoreszentes, Mücken auf Papier
Fluorescent paint, midges on paper
14 × 12 cm

Folgende Seiten / Next pages

13. *Fliegengezwitscher I*, 2006
Stubenfliegen, verschiedene Materialien
Houseflies, mixed media
14 × 12 cm

14. *Fliegengezwitscher II*, 2006
Stubenfliegen, verschiedene Materialien
Houseflies, mixed media
14 × 12 cm

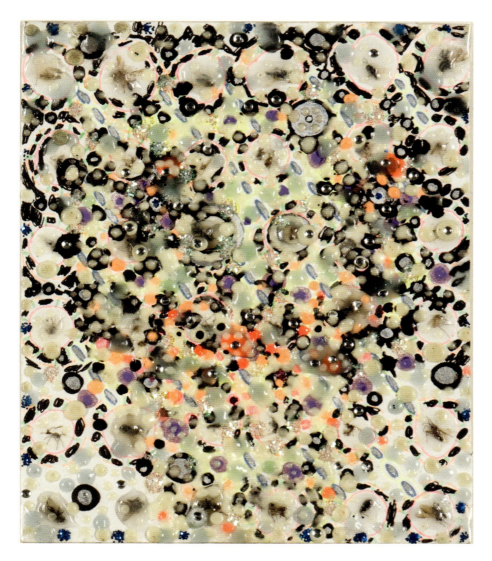

12

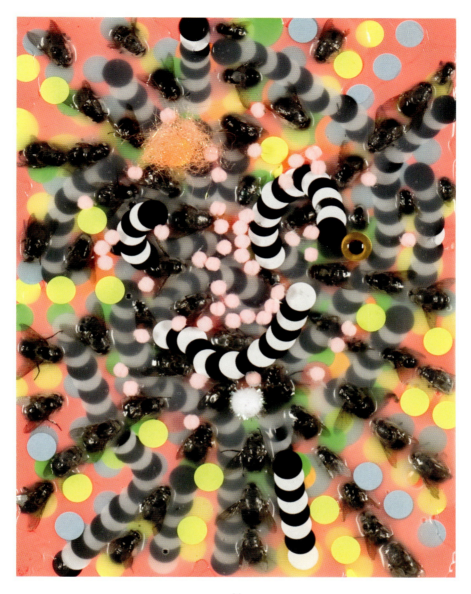

14

15. *Sternmullgeist*, 2006
Maulwurfschädel, verschiedene Materialien
Mole skull, mixed media
17 × 11 cm

BIOAKTIVE SUBJEKTE
BIOACTIVE SUBJECTS

16. *ithyphallic cucumber,* 1999
mit Hausratte / with house rat
Gurke, Buchbinderleim
Cucumber, bookbinding glue
52 × 40 × 36 cm

17

18

17. *Kartoffeltiger,* 2006
mit Ratte / with rat
Buchbinderleim, Kartoffeln, Strass, Toast
Bookbinding glue, potatoes, diamante, toast
14 × 12 × 9 cm

18. *einäugiger Januskopf,* 2008
Buchbinderleim, Salat, Adlerfedern
Bookbinding glue, lettuce, eagle feathers
42 × 20 × 19 cm

19. *Kartoffelkrieger,* 2007
Buchbinderleim, Kartoffeln, verschiedene Materialien
Bookbinding glue, potatoes, mixed media
21 × 27 × 7 cm

19

20. *Dungkrieger,* 2007
Elefantendung, Zement, Alu, Geierflaum
Elephant dung, cement, aluminium, vulture down
89 × 41 × 23 cm

21. *blauer Tod,* 2009
Styropor, Fluoreszentes, Pfauenfedern, Glasaugen,
verschiedene Materialien / Polystyrene, fluorescent paint,
peacock feathers, glass eyes, mixed media
39 × 33 × 17 cm

22. *dreibeinige Eule,* 2007
Kaimanschwanz, Glasaugen, Lack, Plastik auf Plexi
Caiman tail, glass eyes, lacquer, plastic on perspex
32 × 16 × 15 cm

23. *Katze,* 1999
Wolle, Wachs
Wool, wax
9 × 14 × 15 cm

24. *Mäuslesarg,* 2007
Plastik, Gips, Acryl, Lack, Fluoreszentes, Ponpons
Plastic, Plaster, acrylic, lacquer, fluorescent paint,
pompoms
14 × 7 × 13 cm

21

22

23

24

25. *Hasenmond*, 2005
Acryl, Aluminium, Pommes, Hasenfell
Acrylic, aluminium, chips, hare fur
20 × 15 × 3 cm

26. *Fritz's Baumgeist,* 2006
Polyester, Pommes, Ponpons, Glasaugen,
verschiedene Materialien
Polyester, chips, pompoms, glass eyes, mixed media
28 × 18 × 14 cm

27

27. *Ohne Titel,* 2007
Pommes, Buchbinderleim, Heißkleber, Lack,
verschiedene Materialien
Chips, bookbinding glue, hot glue, lacquer, mixed media
37 × 14 × 14 cm

28. *Pommeskapelle,* 2007
Pommes, Heißkleber, Seifenfiguren, verschiedene
Materialien auf Plexi
Chips, hot glue, soap forms, various materials on perspex
25 × 21 × 33 cm

Folgende Doppelseite / Next spread

29. *Heller Baumgeist,* 2007
Menschenhaar, Acryl, Glasaugen
Human hair, acrylic, glass eyes
53 × 20 × 20 cm

30. *Präapokalyptikum / 2. Ordnung,* 2007
Körperbehaarung, verschiedene Materialien
Body hair, mixed media
38 × 11 × 8 cm

28

31. *Beflügelte Spitze*, 2008
Wachs, Plastik, Seife
Wax, plastic, soap
21 × 18 × 15 cm

32. *Bunny M,* 2008
Seife, Ponpon, Holz, Kronentaubenfeder
Soap, pompom, wood, crowned-pigeon feather
20 × 7 × 7 cm

33. *romantische Spaghetti I,* 2008
Spaghetti, Buchbinderleim, Draht, Fluoreszentes
Spaghetti, bookbinding glue, wire, fluorescent paint
40 × 20 × 20 cm

34. *romantische Spaghetti II,* 2008
Spaghetti, Buchbinderleim, Schaumstoff, Fluoreszentes
Spaghetti, bookbinding glue, foam, fluorescent paint
10 × 25 × 15 cm

35. *Elster, denkend,* 2009
Elsterkopf, Trauben, Leim, verschiedene Materialien
Magpie head, grapes, glue, mixed media
20 × 14 × 8 cm

36. *Lilit,* 2009
Tierpräparate verleimt, verschiedene Materialien
Glued animal specimens, mixed media
27 × 10,5 × 10,5 cm

37. *animierter Grund,* 2009
Buchbinderleim, Äpfel, Karotten, Glasaugen,
verschiedene Materialien
Bookbinding glue, apples, carrots, glass eyes, mixed media
39 × 33 × 17 cm

LÄCHLER
SMILER

38. *grüner Lächler*, 2007
Ölpastellkreide auf Papier
Oil pastel on paper
29,5 × 19 cm

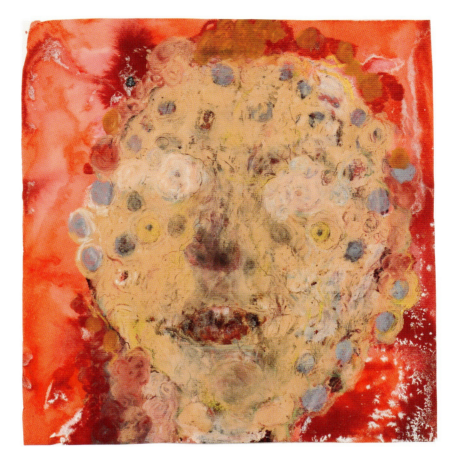

39

40

41

43

44

Vorhergehende Seiten / Previous pages

39. *Lächler Vierauge II,* 2008
Ölwachskreide auf Papier
Oil pastel on paper
24 × 21 cm

40. *Lächler Vierauge I,* 2008
Ölwachskreide auf Papier
Oil pastel on paper
26 × 25 cm

41. *Lächler (Du!),* 2007
Ölpastellkreide auf Papier
Oil pastel on paper
30 × 21 cm

42. *Lächler (Du!),* 2007
Ölpastellkreide auf Papier
Oil pastel on paper
30 × 27 cm

43. *Pink Mond,* 2004
Acryl, Lack auf Leinwand
Acrylic, lacquer on canvas
100 × 80 cm

44. *Lächler argante II,* 2007
Ölwachspastell auf Papier
Oil pastel on paper
28 × 22 cm

45. *Höllenpopanz,* 2006
Acryl, Lack, Öl, Fluoreszentes auf Holz
Acrylic, lacquer, oil, fluorescent paint on wood
32 × 27 cm

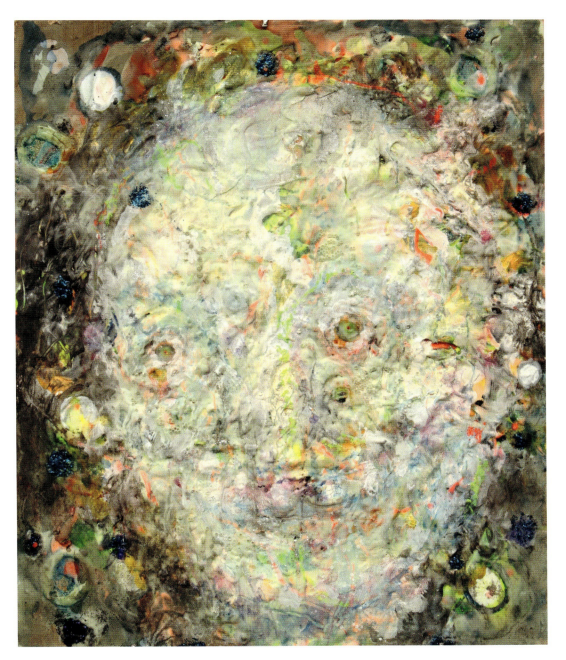
45

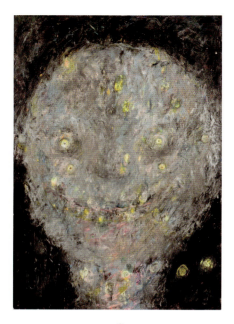

46

47

46. *Lächler Vierauge*, 2006
Ölpastellkreide auf Papier
Oil pastel on paper
40 × 25 cm

47. *dunkla Geist*, 2007
Öl auf Leinwand
Oil on canvas
90 × 90 cm

48. *Lächler*, 2006
Ölpastellkreide auf Papier
Oil pastel on paper
28 × 21 cm

49. *Modder-Lächler*, 2008
Ölwachskreide auf Papier
Oil pastel on paper
28 × 20 cm

48

50

50. *Elephrontal*, 2006
Acryl, Öl auf Pappe
Acrylic, oil on card
79 × 59 cm

51. *Colonel Fabien*, 2007
Aquarell, Lack, Tusche
Watercolour, lacquer, Indian ink
30 × 21 cm

Folgende Doppelseite / Next spread

52. *Wolkenpopanz*, 2007
Ölwachskreide auf Papier
Oil pastel on paper
26 × 17 cm

53. *Sonnenpopanz*, 2007
Ölwachskreide auf Papier
Oil pastel on paper
39 × 29 cm

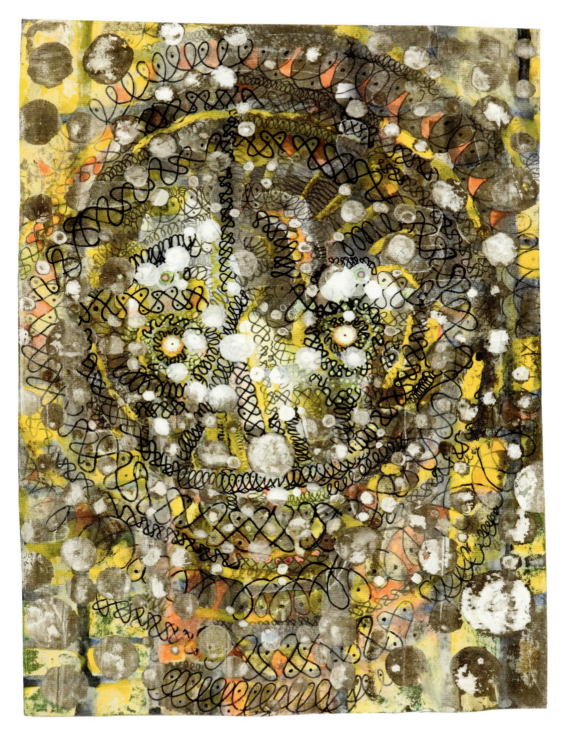

51

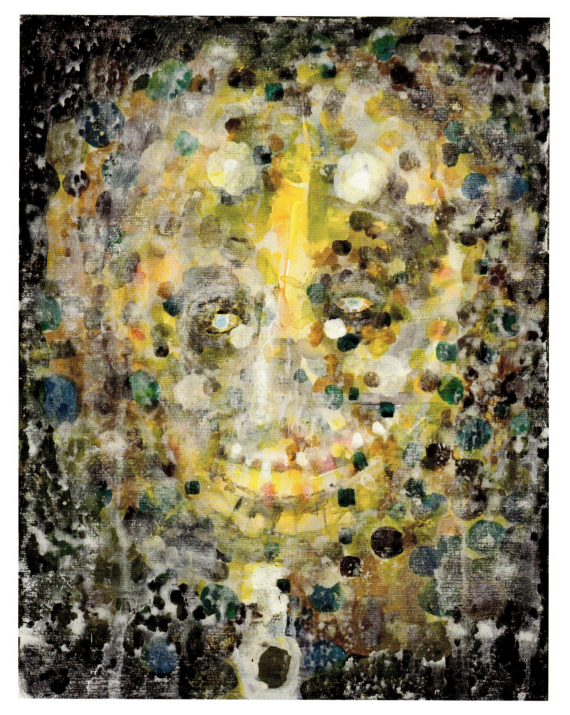
53

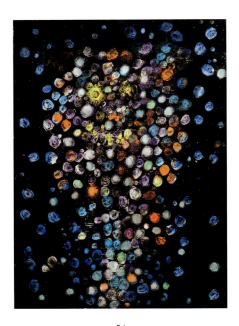

54

55

54. *Punktegeist II,* 2006
Ölwachskreide auf Papier in Plexiglas
Oil pastel on paper in perspex
40 × 28 cm

55. *lächelndes Auge,* 2006
Ölpastellkreide auf Papier
Oil pastel on paper
32,5 × 27 cm

56. *Punktegeist,* 2007
Ölwachskreide auf Papier
Oil pastel on paper
33 × 23 cm

57. *Punktegeist,* 2007
Pastellkreide auf Karton
Pastel on cardboard
56 × 42 cm

56

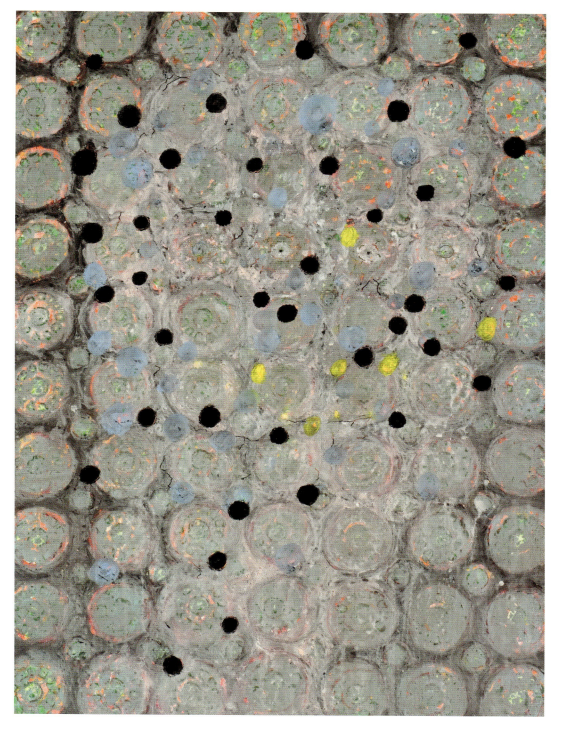

58

59

58. *Hexe Lächlerin,* 2007
Ölwachspastell auf Papier
Oil pastel on paper
31 × 24 cm

59. *Froschgeist,* 2008
Ölwachskreide auf Papier
Oil pastel on paper
30 × 23 cm

60. *Schweinegeist,* 2007
Ölwachskreide auf Papier
Oil pastel on paper
30 × 23 cm

61. *Versaillegeist,* 2007
Ölwachskreide auf Papier
Oil pastel on paper
31 × 22 cm

60

61

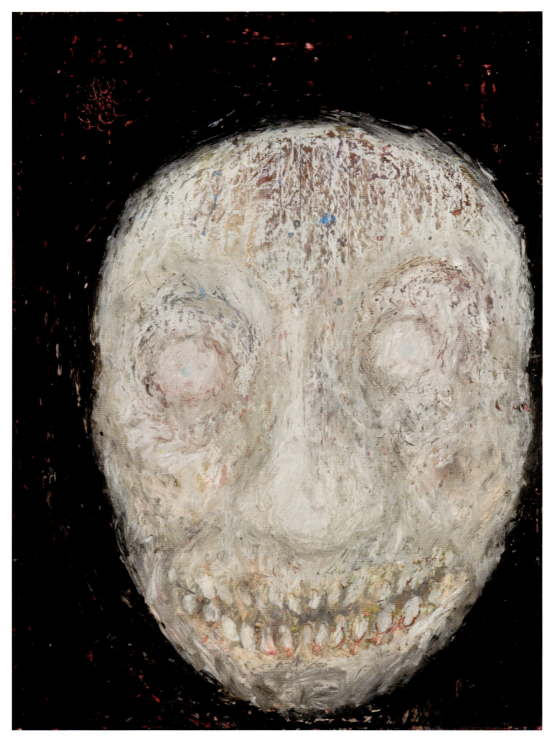

65

Vorhergehende Seiten / Previous pages

62. *Lichtknecht II*, 2008
Ölpastellkreide auf Papier
Oil pastel on paper
30,5 × 20,5 cm

63. *Lichtknecht I*, 2008
Ölpastellkreide auf Papier
Oil pastel on paper
29 × 21 cm

64. *witchbitch*, 2008
Öl, Pastellkreide, Tusche auf Leinwand
Oil, pastel, Indian ink on canvas
54 × 44 cm

65. *witchbitch II*, 2009
mit / with Axel Heil, fluid editions Basel
handpigmentierter Chromalindruck, Zeichnung
Hand-coloured chromalin print, drawing
Auflage / edition: 20
20 × 20 cm

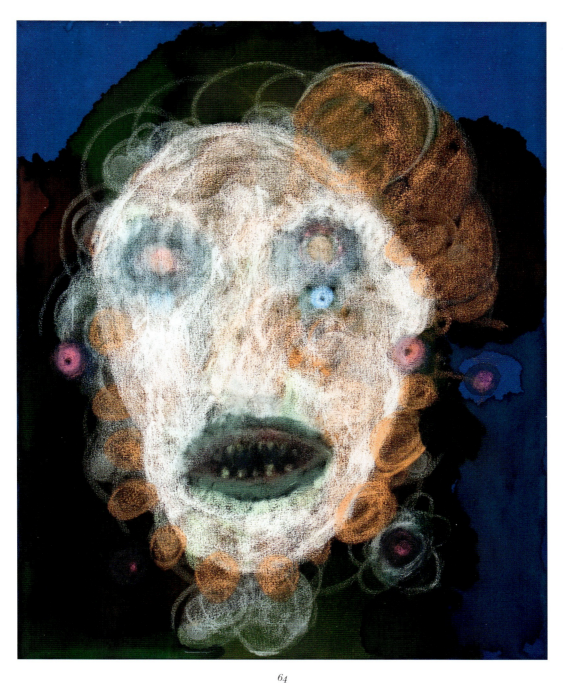

68

69

Vorhergehende Doppelseite / Previous spread

66. *Graupopanz I*, 2009
mit / with Anke Wenzel
Aquarell, Tusche auf Papier
Watercolour, Indian ink on paper
29 × 21 cm

67. *Graupopanz II*, 2009
mit / with Anke Wenzel
Aquarell, Tusche auf Papier
Watercolour, Indian ink on paper
29 × 21 cm

68. *Höllengeistmeinzimani I*, 2008
Acryl, Fluoreszentes, Lack, verschiedene Materialien
Acrylic, fluorescent paint, lacquer, mixed media
28 × 21 cm

69. *gelber Leberlächler*, 2008
Ölwachskreide auf Papier
Oil pastel on paper
29 × 21 cm

70. *Wassergeist*, 2005
verschiedene Materialien auf Folie
Various materials on transparency film
26 × 18 cm

71. *Punktegeist I / 2.Ordnung*, 2009
Papier, Monotypie, Lack
Paper, monotype, lacquer
40 × 29 cm

72. *Punktegeist II / 2.Ordnung*, 2009
Papier, Monotypie, Lack
Paper, monotype, lacquer
40 × 29 cm

70

71

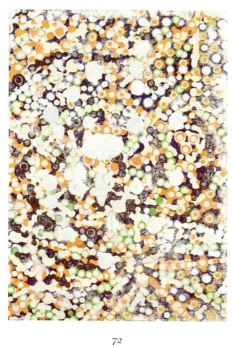

72

73. *Kupferkopf,* 2009
Ölwachskreide auf Papier
Oil pastel on paper
30 × 21 cm

PRÄAPOKALYPTIKUM
PREAPOCALYPTICON

74. *Präapokalyptikum I*, 2001
Neonklebepunkte auf Pappe
Adhesive neon dots on card
76 × 110 cm

75. *Präapokalyptikum III*, 2004
Neonklebepunkte auf Pappe
Adhesive neon dots on card
47 × 66 cm

76. *Präapokalyptikum IV*, 2004
Neonklebepunkte auf Pappe
Adhesive neon dots on card
47 × 66 cm

77. *Präapokalyptikum V*, 2005
Neonklebepunkte auf Pappe
Adhesive neon dots on card
47 × 66 cm

78. *Präapokalyptikum VIII*, 2007
Neonklebepunkte auf Pappe
Adhesive neon dots on card
48 × 68 cm

79. *Präapokalyptikum X*, 2007
Neonklebepunkte auf Pappe
Adhesive neon dots on card
48 × 68 cm

74

75

76

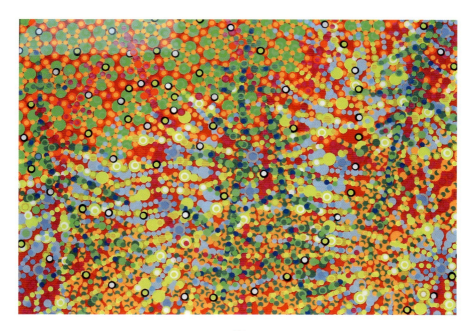

77

78

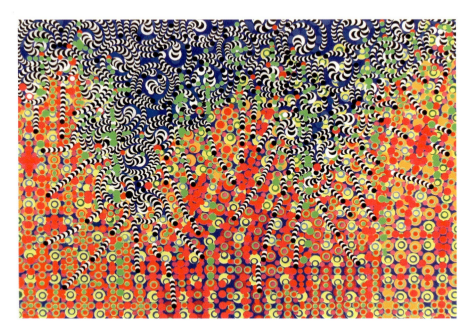

79

RASCHA-RASCHA (KLEINER REGEN)
RASCHA-RASCHA (LITTLE RAIN)

80. *rascha-rascha Somanga II*, 2005
Aquarell auf Pappe
Watercolour on card
30 × 35 cm

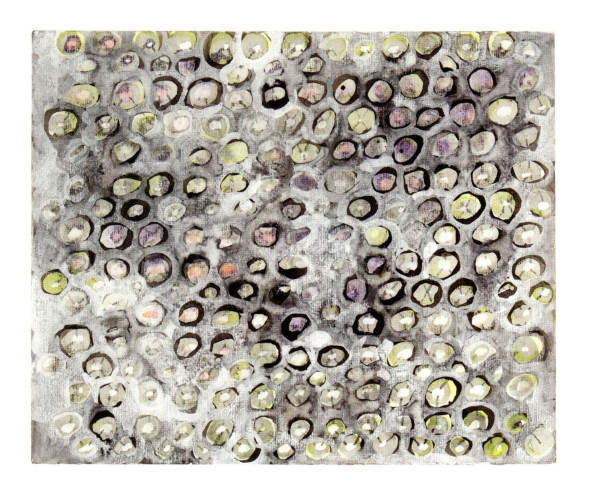

81

81. *Utete*, 2004
Filzstift und Lack auf Papier
Felt pen and lacquer on paper
14 × 21 cm

82. *rascha-rascha Somanga I*, 2005
Aquarell auf Pappe
Watercolour on card
30 × 40 cm

83. *Nguva*, 2004
Lack, Aquarell auf Papier
Lacquer, watercolour on paper
15 × 14 cm

84. *upepo ya kassa*, 2004
Schildpatt, Lack
Tortoise shell, lacquer
7 × 9 cm

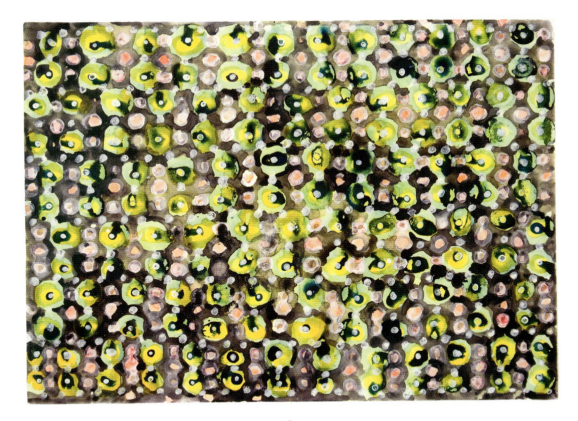

82

83

84

85

86

85. *Somanga*, 2005
Filzstift auf Papier
Felt pen on paper
21 × 15 cm

86. *rascha-rascha I,* 2004
KILWA MASOKO SIRENENHEIME
Filzstift, Aquarell, Lack, Tusche,
Papier auf Pappe aufgezogen
Felt pen, watercolour, lacquer, Indian ink,
paper on cardboard
19 × 14 cm

87. *rascha-rascha (kleiner Regen) II,* 2005
Filzstift, Lack, Aquarell,
Papier auf Pappe aufgezogen
Felt pen, lacquer, watercolour,
paper on cardboard
21 × 14 cm

87

88. *Matema*, 2005
mit / with Anke Wenzel
Acryl auf Leinwand
Acrylic on canvas
120 × 80 cm

89. *rascha-rascha argante,* 2006
Lack auf Folie
Lacquer on transparency film
26 × 18 cm

90. *Rufiji-Geist,* 2005
Aquarell auf Papier
Watercolour on paper
21 × 15 cm

91. *rascha-rascha III,* 2005
Filzstift, Aquarell auf Papier
Felt pen, watercolour on paper
10,5 × 8,5 cm

92. *Bwejuu,* 2005
Tusche auf Papier
Indian ink on paper
21 × 15 cm

89

90

91

92

KLEINE WOLKEN
LITTLE CLOUDS

93. *waoKönig*, 2006
Segeltuch, Glasfaserstäbe, Lack, Fluoreszentes
Sailcloth, glass-fibre rods, lacquer, fluorescent paint
210 × 200 cm

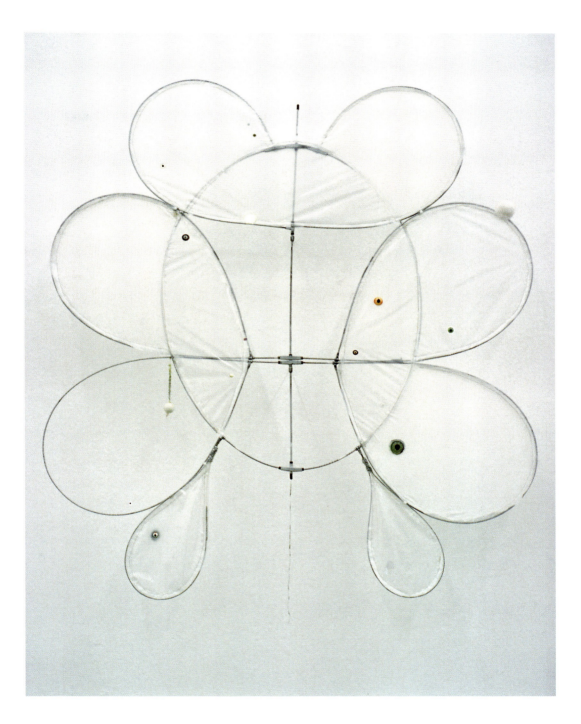

94. *little cloud I*, 2007
mit / with Anke Wenzel
Segeltuch, Kohlefaserstäbe, Glasaugen
Sailcloth, carbon-fibre rods, glass eyes
180 × 160 cm

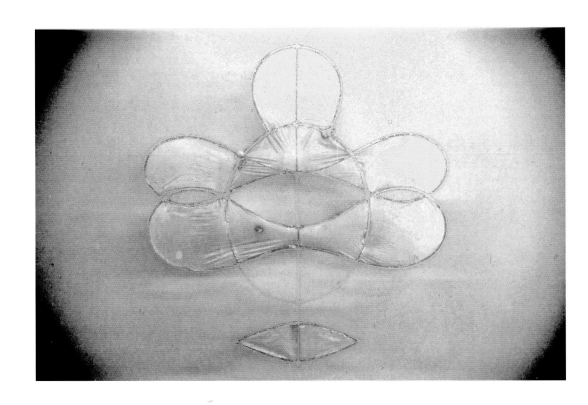

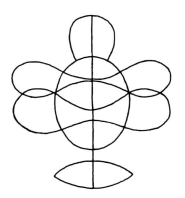

95. *little cloud II*, 2008
mit / with Anke Wenzel
Segeltuch, Kohlefaserstäbe, Windeln
Sailcloth, carbon-fibre rods, nappies
180 × 160 cm

96. *little dark cloud / Motte*, 2008
mit / with Anke Wenzel
Segeltuch, Kohlefaserstäbe
Sailcloth, carbon-fibre rods
180 × 160 × 30 cm

SCHRECKPOPANZE
SCARECROWS

97. *Poplife / vom Nachteil geboren zu sein,* 2007
Holz, Gips, Draht, Lack, Wolle, Fluoreszentes, Stubenfliegen, Glasauge, Spiegel, Bambus, Kokospalmwedel
Wood, plaster of Paris, wire, lacquer, wool, fluorescent paint, houseflies, glass eyes, mirror, bamboo, coconut palm fronds
210 × 60 × 24 cm

98. *Grüner Geist*, 2007
Hausmäuse, Kamelhaar, Ponpons, Fluoreszentes
House mice, camel hair, pompoms, fluorescent paint
30,5 × 26 × 6,5 cm

99. *Steingeist,* 2007
Wismut, Plexi, Lack, verschiedene Materialien
auf Aludibond
Bismuth, perspex, lacquer, mixed media on Aludibond
35 × 21 × 20 cm

100

100. *Theiresiasgeist,* 2007
Glasaugen, Museumskäfer, Buchbinderleim, Plexi, verschiedene Materialien
Glass eyes, museum beetle, bookbinding glue, perspex, mixed media
32 × 22 × 9 cm

101. *Wilder Geist I,* 2008
Mausschädel, Glasaugen, Stubenfliegen auf Plexi
Mouse skull, glass eyes, houseflies on perspex
25,5 × 17,5 cm

102. *Wilder Geist II,* 2008
Plastik, Motte, Glasaugen, Stubenfliegen auf Plexi
Plastic, moths, glass eyes, houseflies on perspex
24 × 17 cm

103. *Wassergeist V,* 2008
Acryl, Plastik, Lack, Fluoreszentes, Glasaugen, Schwärmer
Acrylic, plastic, lacquer, fluorescent paint, glass eyes, hawk moths
30 × 30 × 9 cm

101

102

103

106

107

Vorhergehende Doppelseite / Previous spread

104. *Nesthäckchen,* 2008
Elster, Diamantfasan, Kaiman, Glasauge, Plastik
Magpie, Lady Amherst's Pheasant, caiman,
glass eye, plastic
26 × 25 cm

105. *Vögeligeist,* 2008
Eisvogel, Glasauge, Spaghetti, Buchbinderleim,
Plastikfolie auf Plexi
Kingfisher, glass eye, spaghetti, bookbinding glue,
transparency film on perspex
32 × 28 cm

106. *Mimi,* 2008
Diverse Tierpräparate auf Plexi, verschiedene Materialien
Various animal specimens on perspex, mixed media
31 × 21 cm

107. *Mäuslegeist,* 2006
Neonklebepunkte, Leim, Maus, Mottenflügel, Glasauge,
Ponpons, Fluoreszentes, Glitterfäden
Adhesive neon dots, glue, mouse, moth wings, glass eye,
pompoms, fluorescent paint, glitter threads
24 × 11 cm

108. *little dark mousecloud,* 2008
Stubenfliegenkuchen, Hausmaus, Buchbinderleim,
Ponpons, Plexi, verschiedene Materialien
Housefly cake, house mouse, bookbinding glue,
pompoms, perspex, mixed media
30 × 24 × 7 cm

108

109. *Windschättin*, 2008
Fasanbalg, Fledermaus, Nachtfalter
Pheasant skin, bat, moth
34 × 34 cm

110. *Windschättin II*, 2009
Pfeilschwanzkrebs, Schwärmer, Fuchsschwanz,
verschiedene Materialien
Horseshoe crab, hawk moth, fox tail, mixed media
41 × 29 cm

111. *Sylphe,* 2008
Stubenfliegenkuchen, Speckkäferlarven, Fluoreszentes,
Adlerdaunen, Leim auf Plexi
Housefly cake, carpet beetle larvae, fluorescent paint, eagle
down, glue on perspex
40 × 22 × 6 cm

Folgende Doppelseite / Next spread

112. *Gigi Glücksgeist,* 2009
Ölwachskreide auf Pappe, Kakerlaken,
Babypfeilschwanzkrebs
Oil pastel on card, cockroaches, baby horseshoe crab
69 × 49 cm

113. *Sonnenshowa,* 2009
Acryl, Öl, Fluoreszentes, Schmetterlinge auf Leinwand
Acrylic, oil, fluorescent paint, butterflies on canvas
120 × 80 cm

112

113

114. *Punktegeist IV,* 2008
Neonklebepunkte, verschiedene Materialien auf Plexi
Adhesive neon dots, mixed media on perspex
27 × 25 cm

115. *Schau mir in die Augen, Kleines,* 2009
mit / with Tilmann Haffke
Pappe, Bauschaum, verschiedene Materialien
Card, building foam, mixed media
30 × 24 cm

116. *Babiganushi*, 2008
Kaimanschwanz, Glasaugen, Lack, Plastik auf Plexi
Caiman tail, glass eyes, lacquer, plastic on perspex
25 × 20 × 17 cm

117. *Mexikanisches Gelächter*, 2009
Stiefel, Holz, Styropor
Boots, wood, polystyrene
134 × 35 × 23 cm

118. *Gigi flehmend (Foucaults Lachen)*, 2009
Leinwand, Papier, Schmetterling, Ozelot
Canvas, paper, butterfly, ocelot
101 × 50 cm

SIRENENHEIME
SIREN HOMES

120

121

122

123

124

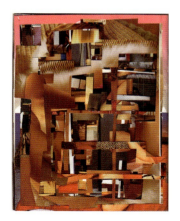

125

126

127

Vorhergehende Seiten / Previous pages

119. *Sirenenheime-Buch,* 1999ff
Totalzensierte Pornohefte
Totally censored pornos
29 × 21 cm

120. *Sirenenheime,* 1999ff
Totalzensierte Pornohefte
Totally censored pornos
32 × 42 cm

121. *Sirenenheime,* 1999ff
Totalzensierte Pornohefte
Totally censored pornos
29 × 22 cm

122. *Sirenenheime,* 1999ff
Totalzensierte Pornohefte
Totally censored pornos
29 × 22 cm

123. *Sirenenheime-Buch,* 1999ff
Totalzensierte Pornohefte
Totally censored pornos
28 × 21 cm

124. *Sirenenheime,* 1999ff
Totalzensierte Pornohefte
Totally censored pornos
22 × 29 cm

125. *Sirenenheime,* 1999ff
Totalzensierte Pornohefte
Totally censored pornos
29 × 22 cm

126. *Sirenenheime,* 1999ff
Totalzensierte Pornohefte
Totally censored pornos
28 × 21 cm

127. *Sirenenheime,* 1999ff
Totalzensierte Pornohefte
Totally censored pornos
24 × 34 cm

Rechte Seite / Right page

128. *Sirenenheime,* 1999ff
Totalzensierte Pornohefte
Totally censored pornos
29 × 43 cm

129. *Sirenenheime,* 1999ff
Totalzensierte Pornohefte
Totally censored pornos
24 × 34 cm

130. *Sirenenheime,* 1999ff
Totalzensierte Pornohefte
Totally censored pornos
32 × 45 cm

Folgende Seiten / Next pages

131. *Sirenenheime,* 1999ff
Totalzensierte Pornohefte
Totally censored pornos
34 × 24 cm

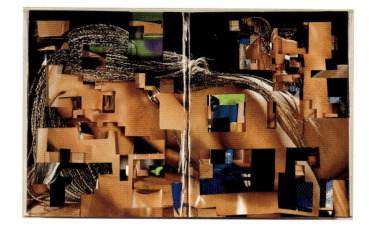

128

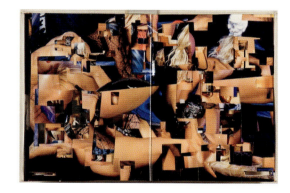

129

130

131

132. *Micronudes*, seit / since 2008
Minutie mit Papierausschnitt, Plexiglas
Minutiae with paper cutout, perspex
31 × 24,5 × 5,5 cm

133.–136. *Seltene Paradiesvorstellung I–IV*, 2009
mit / with Helmut Reinisch
Micronudes auf gewebtem Kelim aus Ketschi (Ziegenhaar)
Micronudes on woven kilim made of ketschi (goat hair)
160 × 126 cm, 190 × 129 cm, 140 × 120 cm, 169 × 118 cm

133

134

135

136

TRANSGRESSION EXZESS
TRANSGRESSION EXCESS

137. *Schimmelschimmel*, 1999
2116 quadratische Petrischalen, Agar-Agar
2116 square petri dishes, agar
2 × 345 × 345 cm

In Kooperation mit Simon Wunderlich im Rahmen des Projektes Mikrokulturen. *Zur Eröffnung der Ausstellung blühten 17 verschiedene Schimmelpilzkulturen.*

In collaboration with Simon Wunderlich as part of the Mikrokulturen *project. The 17 mildew cultures flourished to coincide with the opening of the exhibition.*

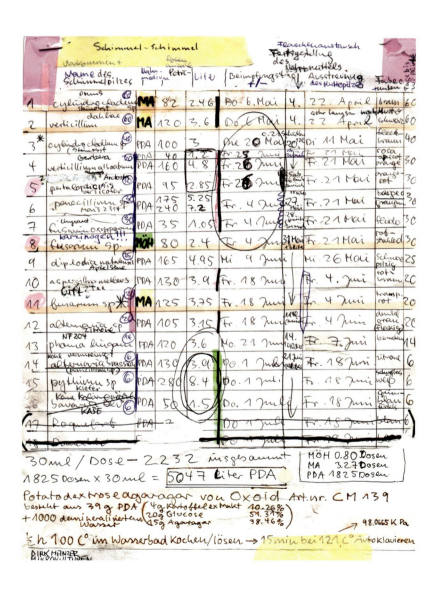

138. *Fibrio Fischerie*, 2003
Leuchtbakterienzucht in verschiedenen Streifen
Plexiglas, Agar-Agar, Bakterien
Luminous bacteria cultures in perspex strips,
agar, bacteria
4 × 50 × 50 cm

139. *Lactowrestling*, 1999
Video and C-prints
6 min

In Kooperation mit Simon Wunderlich im Rahmen des Projektes Mikrokulturen. *Quadratischer Kampfring, 4 × 4 m, 900 Yoghurtkegelstümpfe, schwarze Teichfolie. 3,5 Stunden Marathonwrestling.*

In collaboration with Simon Wunderlich as part of the Mikrokulturen *project. Square wrestling ring, 4 × 4 m, 900 yoghurt frustums, black pond liner. 3.5 hours of marathon wrestling.*

140

140.–146. *Rhizomorphe Landschaften I–VII*, 2003
C-print
42 × 29,7 cm

Die rhizomorphen Landschaften *gehen auf Dias von vergänglichen Objekten zurück. Die Dias werden mit Schimmelpilzen beimpft.*

The rhizomorphe Landschaften *are based on slides of perishable items. The slides are inoculated with mildew.*

141

142

143

144

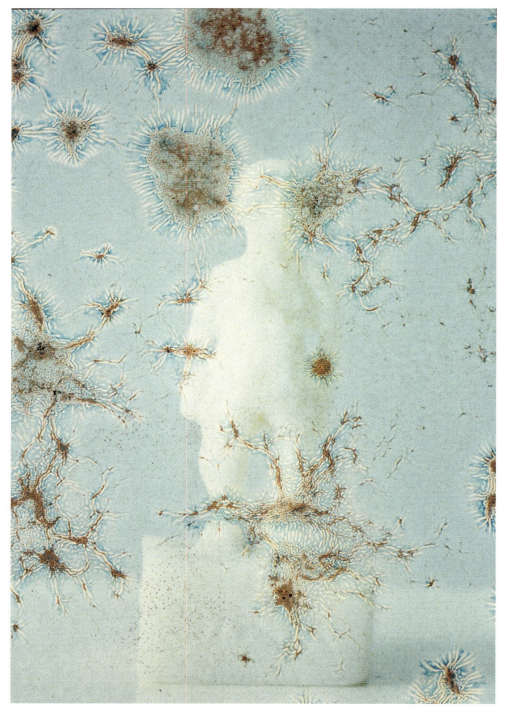
145

146

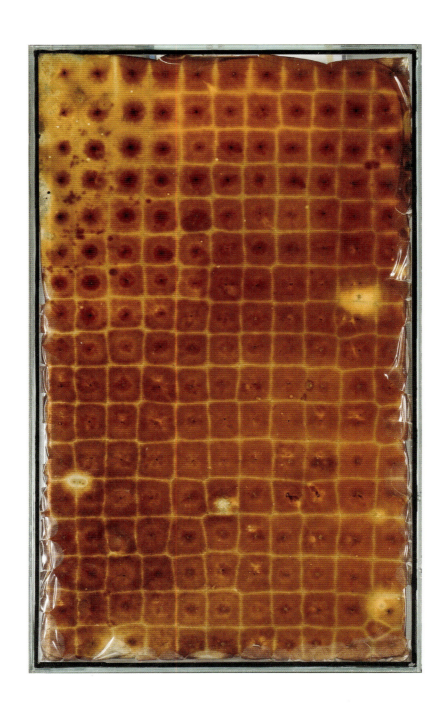

147. *fusarium culmorum*, 2004
Agar-Agar, Schimmelpilz, Glas
Agar, mildew, glass
80 × 50 × 4 cm

148. *botryodiplodia*, 2004
Agar-Agar, Schimmelpilz, Glas
Agar, mildew, glass
80 × 50 × 4 cm

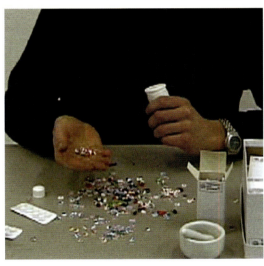

149. *Tannenbaum weiss meinzman*, 2001
Video
46 min

150. *Flying Pieces*, 2007
mit / with Peter Stoffel aka blizzers
Video
1:11 min

151. *Schaumweilen*, 2000
Video
32 min

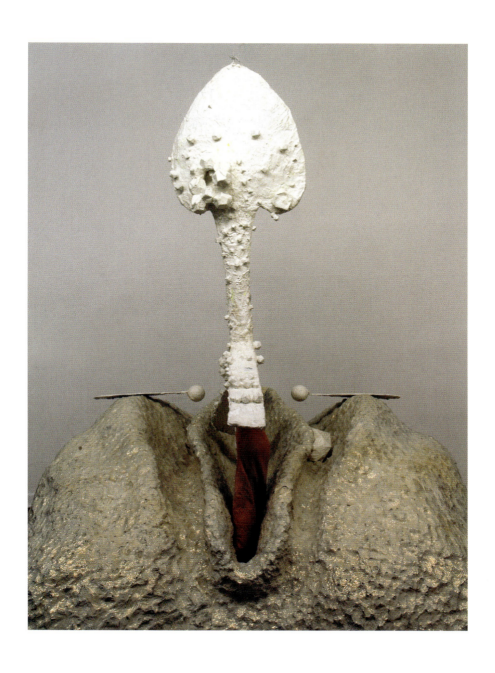

152. *Schaumweile I,* 2000
Schaumstoff, Latex
Foam, latex
180 × 180 × 90 cm

153. *Billy's witch*, 2001
Schaumstoff, Latex, medizinische Pumpe,
Soundsystem, Gleitmittelspringbrunnen
Foam, latex, medical pump, sound system,
lubricant fountain
220 × 140 × 140 cm

Im Rahmen der re-mir-II-*Ausstellung wurde ein hohles Schaumstoff-Latex-Objekt gezeigt, das von einem Pränatal-Fetischisten im Jahr 2000 in Auftrag gegeben wurde. Zur Realisierung dieses Projektes wurde die* easy-easy foundation *gegründet. In das Objekt sind ein Soundsystem und eine medizinische Kreislaufpumpe für Gleitmittel integriert. Das Gleitmittel ermöglicht den Einstieg in* Billy's witch. *Der Innenraum besteht aus einem eiförmigen Zweikammernsystem. Die erste Kammer ist eine fünfzackige Sternformation, deren Zacken vertikal verlaufen. Diese mündet in einen körpergroßen Aufriss. Die sich anschließende zweite Kammer ist eine sechszackige geschraubte Hohlkörperformation. In ihrem Inneren kann eine Person Platz finden und eine kardiophone Symphonie hören.*

The re-mir-II *exhibition included a foam-and-latex work that a prenatal fetishist commissioned in 2000. The easy-easy foundation was founded to help bring this project to life. A sound system and a medical circulation pump for lubricant were integrated into the work. The lubricant facilitates entry into* Billy's witch. *The inner room comprises an oval-shaped dual-chamber-system. The first chamber is a star with five vertical points, which ends in a human-sized hole. The adjoining second chamber is a six-pointed, screwed hollow structure with room for one person to go inside and listen to a cardiophone symphony.*

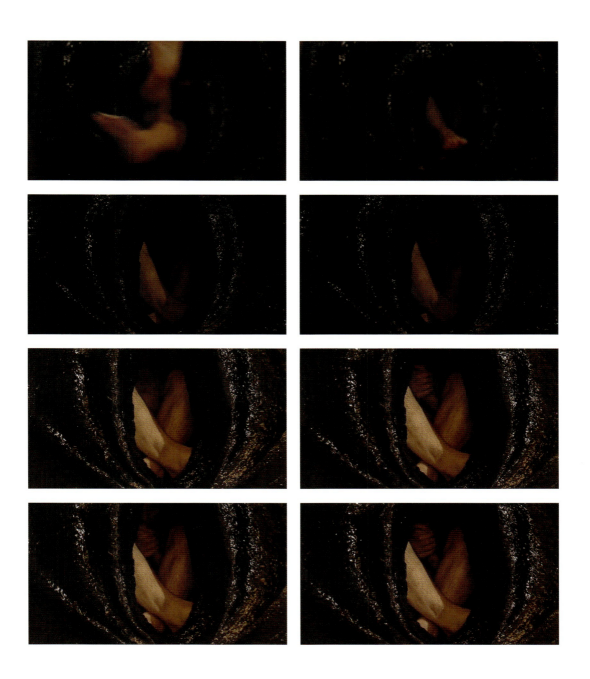

154. *Billy's Brunnengesänge*, 2001
mit / with easy-easy foundation
Video and C-print
9 min

155. *Sirenenheime III*, 2006
Kokospalmwedelflechtwerk, Bambus, Kokosfaser,
innen: Skulptur *Schaumweile V*
Woven coconut palm fronds, bamboo, coconut-fibre,
inside: *Schaumweile V* sculpture
180 × 120 × 240 cm

156. *Schaumweile V*, 2008
Schaumstoff, Alustab
Foam, aluminium pole
165 × 25 × 60 cm

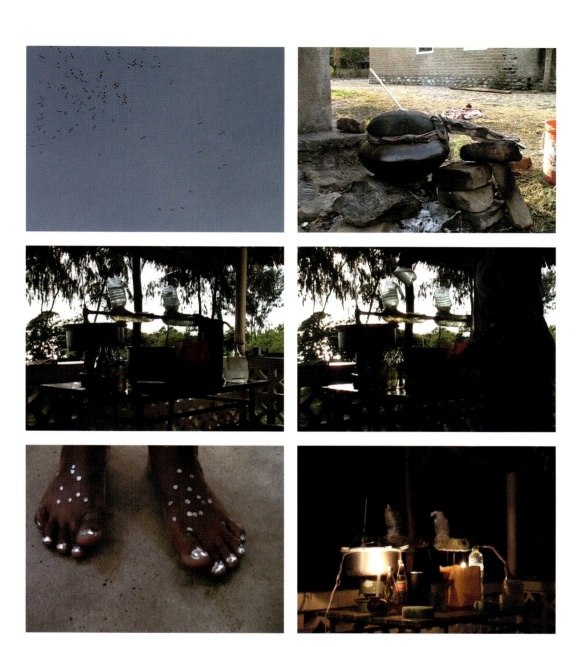

157. *Tränen der Sirenen*, 2006
Video and C-print
11 min

158. *Tabulabor*, 2004
Chemische Destille, verschiedene Materialien
Distillery, mixed media

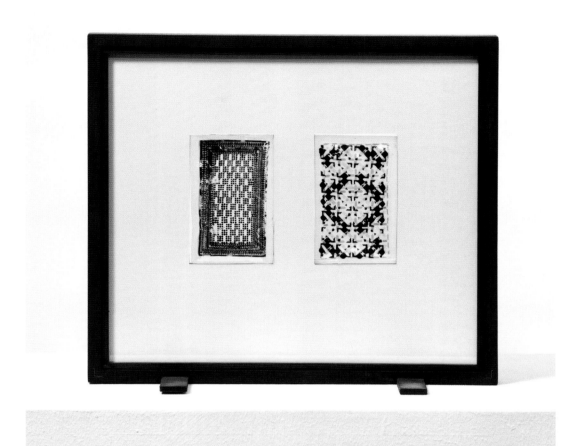

159. *Tränen der Sirenen*, 2004
mit / with Anke Wenzel
PE-Folie, Siebdruck, Schnaps,
Polyethylene film, screenprint, schnaps
6 × 10 cm

160. *Megaron*, 2009
MDF, Latex, Gurken, Schaumstoff auf Leinwand
MDF, latex, cucumber, foam on canvas
180 × 120 × 240 cm

161. *symphatikus boheme*, 2006
Zwölf Zaunelemente aus Holz, Scharnieren,
Rollen, Acryllack
Twelve wooden fence elements, hinges,
wheels, acrylic paint
Höhe / height 120 cm

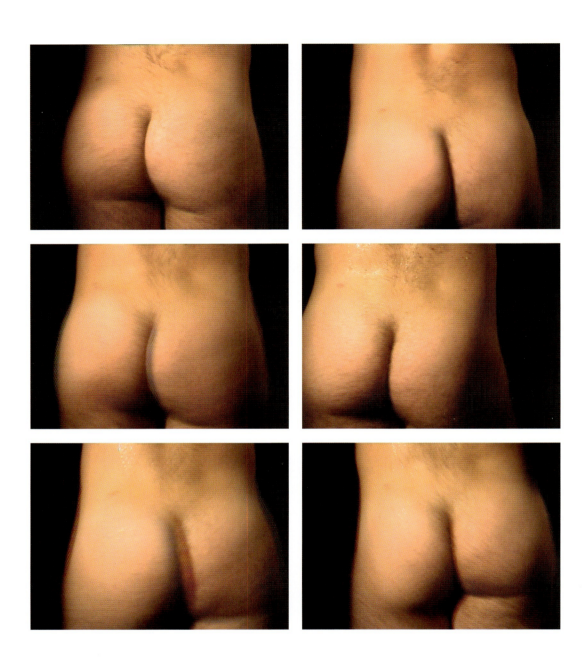

162. *Papa Wata*, 2005
Video
45 min

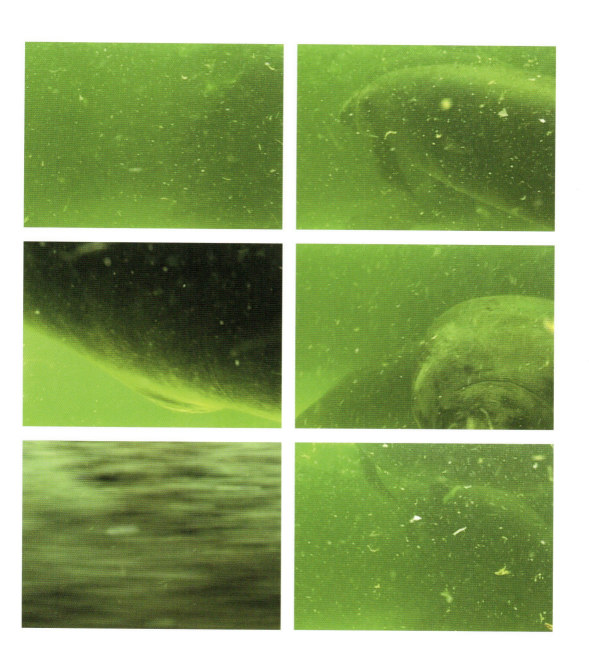

163. *Mami Wata*, 2006
Video
12 min

ANDERE
OTHERS

164. *treeghost*, 2008
Aquarell auf Papier
Watercolour on paper
39 × 30 cm

165. *Stufen der Wandlung*, 2005
mit / with Anke Wenzel
Mundgeblasenes Glas
Blown glass

166

166. *Palmepiphanie II*, 2006
Aluminium
45 × 3 × 90 cm

167. *Urkunde I*, 2004
Filzstift auf Papier
Felt pen on paper
25 × 20 cm

168. *Urkunde II*, 2004
Filzstift auf Papier
Felt pen on paper
18 × 38 cm

Folgende Doppelseite / Next spread

169. *Dugong Mansesse I–IV*, 2004
Fotografie
Photography
84 × 119 cm

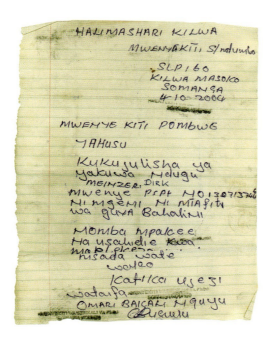

167

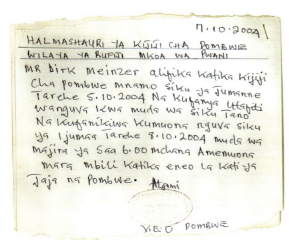

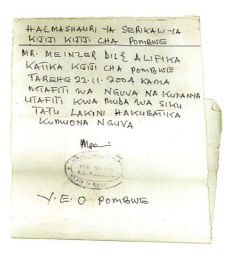

168

TEXTE
TEXTS

Annett Reckert
Wenn die Vernunft schläft, singen die Sirenen

Dirk Meinzer ist ein Feldforscher im Reich der Sirenen, jener Bestrickerinnen, die als archetypische Mischwesen in den Mythologien aller Kulturen anzutreffen sind. Er selbst beschreibt sie als „lockende Verkünderinnen einer anderen Welt, sie verführen Reisende zum Verweilen, zum Wahnsinn, zum Tod. Sie sitzen an der Grenze zum Unbekannten, zum Paradies, an fremden Gärten, singen Spiegellieder und inspirieren zur Entdeckung der eigenen Besessenheit."[1] In der Ausstellung *Sirenenheime* gastieren sie in einem Panoptikum, das an die Kunst- und Wunderkammern der Spätrenaissance und des Barock denken lässt. Jede Ecke und Windung der labyrinthischen Schau lässt das Publikum staunen; zugleich steht die Frage nach der Herkunft und Ordnung der Dinge im Raum. Auf der Suche nach einer Antwort mag die Assemblage *Gigi flehmend*, 2009 – ein zähnebleckender Hybridgaul, der aus einem prächtigen Eulenfalter und einem Ozelotfell erwachsen ist – daran erinnern, dass nicht nur das Staunen sondern auch das Lachen erkenntnisstiftend sein kann.

So ist Michel Foucaults Lachen bei der Lektüre eines Textes von Jorge Luis Borges legendär geworden; es war der Impuls für seine 1966 erschienene Schrift *Die Ordnung der Dinge*, in der er unter anderem radikal die Tragfähigkeit klassischer raum-zeit-gebundener Taxonomien hinterfragte. Bei Jorge Luis Borges ist die Rede von einer „gewisse[n] chinesische[n] Enzyklopädie". Diese kategorisiert wie folgt „a) Tiere, die dem Kaiser gehören, b) einbalsamierte Tiere, c) gezähmte, d) Milchschweine, e) Sirenen, f) Fabeltiere, g) herrenlose Hunde, h) in diese Gruppierung gehörige, i) die sich wie Tolle gebärden, j) unzählbare, k) die mit einem ganz feinen Pinsel aus Kamelhaar gezeichnet sind, l) und so weiter, m) die den Wasserkrug zerbrochen haben, n) die von weitem wie Fliegen aussehen."[2] Michel Foucault kommentiert selbst: „Bei dem Erstaunen über diese Taxonomie erreicht man mit einem Sprung, was in dieser Aufzählung uns als der exotische Zauber eines anderen Denkens bezeichnet wird – die Grenze unseres Denkens: die schiere Unmöglichkeit, *das* zu denken."[3] Dieser Kommentar wie auch die Bizarrie der fiktiven Systematik von Jorge Luis Borges selbst haben mit Blick auf Dirk Meinzers Sirenenkosmos keinen schlechten Klang. Vielmehr ermuntert beides zu einer ‚wilden' Kategorisierung, die von dem Bild und den Bildern einer Ausstellung erzählt – und im gleichen Zuge von der Geburt der Sirenologie aus dem Geist der Transgression. Dabei erweist

Annett Reckert
When reason sleeps, the sirens sing

Translation by Jenny Metcalf

Dirk Meinzer conducts field research in the realm of the sirens, those characteristic hybrid enchantresses that one encounters in the myths of cultures everywhere. Dirk Meinzer describes them as "alluring harbingers of another world, who entice travellers into staying, into madness, into death. They wait on the threshold of the unknown, of paradise, of exotic lands, singing mirror songs that force passers-by to confront their own obsessions."[1] These mythical creatures feature in *Siren Homes*, a collection reminiscent of Late-Renaissance and Baroque cabinets of curiosities. Every twist and turn of this labyrinthine exhibition leaves viewers amazed and questioning the origins and arrangement of the items on display. While searching for answers, a glance at *Gigi Flehming*, 2009 – an assemblage depicting a teeth-baring hybrid nag fashioned from a magnificent owlet moth and an ocelot pelt – may very well serve as a reminder that laughter, as much as amazement, can be enlightening.

118

This is why Michel Foucault's laughter when reading a text by Jorge Luis Borges has become legendary – the incident provided the inspiration for his 1966 book, *The Order of Things*, in which he radically explored, among other things, the tenability of traditional time-space-bound taxonomies. Jorge Luis Borges talks of "a certain Chinese encyclopaedia", which sets out the following categories of animal: "a) those that belong to the emperor, b) embalmed ones, c) those that are trained, d) suckling pigs, e) sirens, f) fabulous ones, g) stray dogs, h) those included in the present classification, i) those that tremble as if mad, j) innumerable, k) those that are drawn with a very fine camel-hair brush, l) etcetera, m) those that have just broken the water jug, n) those that look like flies from a long way off."[2] Michel Foucault commented on this as follows: "In the wonderment of this taxonomy, the thing we apprehend in one great leap, the thing that, by means of the fable, is demonstrated as the exotic charm of another system of thought, is the limitation of our own, the stark impossibility of thinking that."[3] Foucault's

1

observation and the bizarreness of Borges' fictitious system resonate rather well with Dirk Meinzer's siren world. In fact, both encourage a 'random' categorization that describes the image and the pictures in the exhibition – while at the same time explaining how the spirit of transgression gave birth

II

sich Dirk Meinzers Sirenologie als ein weit gespanntes Forschungsfeld, das Entdeckungen im Alltäglichen und auf Reisen, in der Kunst-, Literatur- und Wissenschaftsgeschichte, in der eigenen Biographie, in der Wirklichkeit, im Traum und im Vorbewussten verspricht.

Mit rauschhafter Heiterkeit tanzt Dirk Meinzer über seine Forschungsfelder hinweg, überschreitet er auf der Suche nach noch unerkannten, gefährlichen Verlockungen immer wieder neugierig und wagemutig die Grenzen dieser Felder. Ebenso gehört die Überschreitung der eigenen Rolle als Schöpfer und Autor zum Konzept. Viele Arbeiten entstehen durch ein kongeniales Zuspiel zwischen Künstlern und Künstlerinnen, allen voran Anke Wenzel. Wie ein betörender Rattenfänger zieht Dirk Meinzer zudem je nach Projekt immer wieder Experten, Spezialisten und Freaks unterschiedlicher Couleur in sein Leben und Schaffen.

Finden Dirk Meinzers Arbeiten in einer Ausstellung zusammen, so gerät diese zu einer orgiastischen Feier im Hier und Jetzt, die zugleich dem Spirituellen augenzwinkernd Einlass gewährt. Dabei zeigen sich bildmächtige Lokalisierungen: die samt und sonders von Dirk Meinzer so benannten

a) Sirenenheime

Sie bilden einen eigenwilligen temporären Wohnpark, der den Besucher bei seinem Rundgang an den etymologisch engen Zusammenhang von Heim und heimlich bzw. geheim (althochdeutsch: zum Haus gehörig, vertraut) erinnern mag. Schließlich würden die Sirenen Dirk Meinzers ihrem Ruf nicht gerecht, wenn sie nicht das ein oder andere Geheimnis hüten würden. Dennoch schaffen sie unterschiedlich dimensionierte Sphären, Sektoren und Zonen, durch die sich das Publikum bewegen kann und so fühlt sich ein jeder eingeladen in mehr oder minder belebte *Sirenenheime*, in zeichnerisch oder faktisch angelegte Gärten und Habitate zu spähen, in Quartiere,

to sirenology. Thus, Dirk Meinzer's sirenology proves to be a series of vast fields of research that hold the promise of discoveries in everyday life and while travelling, in art, literary and scientific history, in his own past, and in dreams and preconsciousness.

Dirk Meinzer leads a vibrant, exhilarating dance across every corner of every field, and on his quest for hidden, dangerous temptations he transcends the fields' boundaries, fuelled by a never-ending sense of curiosity and adventure. His concept is also about transcending his own role as a creator and author – for several of the works in the collection, he affably passed the baton on to other artists, most notably Anke Wenzel. Like an artistic pied piper, Dirk Meinzer invariably entices all manner of experts, specialists and enthusiasts into his projects and his life.

When Dirk Meinzer brings his works together in an exhibition, he creates an orgiastic party in the here and now – but also ushers in the spiritual world with a twinkle in his eye. The revellers form visually striking groups – and Dirk Meinzer has a name for all of them:

a) Siren Homes

These create a unique, temporary residential area that reflects the close etymological ties between the German words *Heim* (home) and *heimlich* (secret) or *geheim* (Old High German, meaning 'of the house', or 'intimate'). After all, Dirk Meinzer's sirens would hardly live up to their reputation if they did not conceal a secret or two. Nonetheless, they create spheres, sectors and zones of different dimensions through which the public are free to wander. Viewers have a sense of being invited into these *siren homes* – some highly animated, others less so – to peer into drawn or actual gardens and habitats; into living spaces, cabinets, boxes and chests; into picture frames and mirrors; into every nook and cranny. All manner of simple dwellings are open to the inquisitive eye and some call to mind small temples, chapels or graves.

The *Saturnopticon* was built for the Kunsthalle Göppingen in 2009. This [1] complex architectural structure is a large, walk-in icosahedron made of wood and white vapour-barrier foil. The foil forms the outer shell of this unconventional sacred building, a function that all but obscures its unholy origins.

Plato's natural philosophy assigns the four elements a central role and theorizes that the icosahedron is water's smallest, indivisible geometric structural element, making it the perfect dwelling for those born of the sea. By the same token, however, it also exemplifies the sirens' deceitfulness and destructive powers – microbiologists and epidemiologists have long known that many viruses share this geometric structure.

Kabinette, Kästen und Objekte, in Bildgevierte und Spiegel, in sämtliche Winkel und Ecken. In allerlei urwüchsige Hütten und Behausungen ist zu lugen; mancherorts stellt sich die Assoziation einer kleinen Tempelanlage, einer Kapelle oder eines Grabmals ein.

Eine komplexe Architektur ist das 2009 für die Kunsthalle Göppingen realisierte *Saturnoptikum*, ein großer begehbarer Ikosaeder aus Holz und weißer Dampfbremsfolie. Als Außenhaut dieses eigenwilligen Sakralbaus macht letztere ihre profane Herkunft allerdings nahezu vergessen.

In der platonischen Naturphilosophie, in der die vier Elemente eine zentrale Rolle spielen, wird auf den Ikosaeder als kleinstes, unteilbares geometrisches Strukturelement des Wassers spekuliert. Natürlich qualifiziert vor allem dies ihn als Heim der Schaumgeborenen. Im gleichen Zuge verweist er auf deren Hinterhältigkeit und Zerstörungskraft. Schließlich ist der Ikosaeder für den Mikrobiologen und Epidemiologen ein altbekannter Virenbauplan.

Wer Dirk Meinzers *Saturnoptikum* betritt, mag vorübergehend seiner zwischen Raum und Fläche oszillierenden Wahrnehmung erliegen. Dieses Verwirrspiel wird durch die Absorption der Schritte auf einem heimeligen Teppich und durch ein diffuses, fast lähmendes Licht konterkariert. Sekunden später entpuppt sich der aus 20 gleichseitigen Dreiecken bestehende Bau noch dazu als eine raffinierte architektonische Gelenkstelle, die jedem Gast eine Entscheidung abverlangt. Wohin auch immer er sich wendet, deutet sich etwas an, was zunächst nicht unbedingt vertraut ist: ein sternförmiges Spiegelkabinett, ein abenteuerliches Destillenlabor, die Wand einer Kokospalmwedelhütte, das numinose Grün von Unterwasseraufnahmen. Letzteres führt zu der einzigen tatsächlich in einem Bild, in filmisch dokumentierenden Bildern, zu bannenden Erscheinungsform

b) der Sirenae, der Seekühe

Es handelt sich um eine Ordnung der Huftiere, der die Anpassung an das Wasserleben gelungen ist. Die Sirenae sind eine Gattung von gewaltigen trägen Meeressäugetieren, die bis zu vier Meter lang und 1000 Kilogramm schwer werden können. Die bereits im 18. Jahrhundert ausgerottete Stellersche Seekuh, benannt nach ihrem Entdecker Georg Wilhelm Steller, erreichte sogar eine Länge von bis zu 7½ Metern.

Die Sirenae stehen den Elefanten nahe, grasen aber ohne Unterlass und damit eher kuhaffin auf den Unterwasserweiden tropischer Gewässer, um tagein tagaus ihren immensen Appetit zu stillen. Zu unterscheiden sind Rundschwanz-Sirenen, zu denen die Manati gehören, und die Gabel-

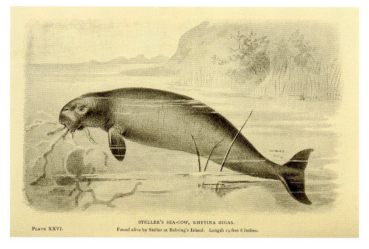

PLATE XXVI.   STELLER'S SEA-COW, RHYTINA GIGAS.
Found alive by Steller at Behring's Island. Length 19 feet 6 inches.

III

Visitors entering Dirk Meinzer's *Saturnopticon* are likely to be temporarily overwhelmed as their senses struggle to separate surface from space. But the confusion subsides when they step onto a plush, homey carpet, and take in the diffuse, almost paralysing light. Seconds later, the structure, which is made up of 20 equilateral triangles, becomes a sophisticated architectural junction that demands a decision of each and every one of its guests. Whatever choice they make, they are greeted with sights that may at first seem unfamiliar: a star-shaped hall of mirrors, a fascinating distillery, the wall of a hut made of coconut palm fronds or the numinous green of underwater images. This last sight leads to documentary footage showing the only manifestation to be actually captured as an image.

b) *Sirenians, sea cows*

This class refers to an order of hoofed mammals that has evolved to be able to live underwater. Sirenians are a species of large, slow-moving sea mammals that can grow up to four metres long and weight as much as 1,000 kilograms. Although it has been extinct since the 18th century, the Steller's sea cow, named after its discoverer Georg Wilhelm Steller, could reach lengths of up to 7½ metres.

Sirenians are closely related to elephants, but they are more bovine in nature since they graze continuously, day in day out, on underwater willows in tropical seas to satisfy their enormous appetites. Two types of sirenians exist: round-tailed sirenians such as the manatee, and the only fork-tailed sirenian, the dugong. Dirk Meinzer went in search of dugongs on his sirenological expeditions. Handwritten, stamped documents of varying authenticity

167-168

167, 168 schwanz-Sirenen mit ihrer einzigen Art, dem Dugong. Letztere hat Dirk Meinzer auf seinen sirenologischen Expeditionen gesucht. Mit mehr oder minder überzeugender Beweiskraft berichten davon handschriftlich in Swahili verfasste und mit Stempeln versehene Dokumente von tansanischen Dorfältesten. Als traurigen Ersatz für seine fehlgeschlagenen Bemühungen in freier Wildbahn hat Dirk Meinzer einen beherzten Tauchgang in das Manati-Becken des Tierpark Berlin-Friedrichsfelde gewagt. Dort ist 2006

163 das 12-minütige Video *Mami wata* entstanden: ein hypnotisierender Blick in eine trübe Ursuppe, in der sich borstige Manati atemberaubend nah zeigen. In Anbetracht der heranwabernden Leibwalzen ist Tiervater Alfred Brehm beizupflichten, wenn er resümiert: „Wer bei den Sirenen der Tierkundigen an jene Märchengestalten des Altertums denken wollte, welche, halb Weib,

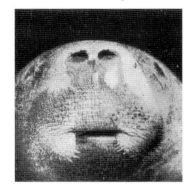

IV

halb Fisch, die krystallenen Wogen des Meeres bewohnen und den armen Erdensohn durch wunderbaren Gesang und noch wunderbarere Gebärden, durch Neigen des Hauptes und glühende Blicke der Augen einladen, zu ihnen hinabzusteigen, mit ihnen zu spielen, zu kosen und – zu verderben, würde sich irren. […] Es gehört lebhafte Einbildungskraft dazu, in diesen Tieren, selbst wenn sie auch in weiter Ferne sich zeigen sollten, Seejungfrauen zu erblicken: mit dem schönen Leib des Menschenweibes haben die plumpen, ungeschlachten Tiere bloß insofern etwas gemein, als die Zitzen auch bei ihnen an der Brust (zwischen den Vorderflossen) liegen und nach Art von Brüsten mehr als bei anderen Seesäugern hervortreten."[4] Damit ist für eine weitere zentrale, den Meinzer'schen Kosmos erschließende Kategorie das Stichwort gefallen. Es geht um

c) Sirenen, für deren Wahrnehmung
„lebhafte Einbildungskraft" wenn auch nicht notwendig
so doch in jedem Fall hilfreich ist

Dirk Meinzer arbeitet besessen an den Oberflächen der Dinge; dort lauern die wahren Verführungen im Detail. Ein solcher in der westlichen Kulturkritik vielfach geradezu moralisch diffamierter Oberflächenfetischismus erschafft erst die Schauplätze, an denen sich die Phantasien der Betrachter entfesseln. Diese beeindrucken keineswegs durch ihre Ausmaße; nicht selten sind es dichte Miniaturen, die aus intimster Nähe betrachtet werden wollen. Noch dazu verweist mancher Titel auf die Liebe zur kleinen Form und dabei

24 erweisen Arbeiten, die zum Beispiel *Mäuslesarg*, 2007 oder *Männle auf Brache*, 2007 heißen, dem süddeutschen Diminutiv eine Referenz.

produced in Swahili by Tanzanian village elders make mention of this creature. His attempts in the wild failed, but Dirk Meinzer refused to be discouraged and, although a somewhat sorry substitute, he went on to dive with the manatees at the Friedrichsfelde zoo in Berlin. It was here in 2006 that he shot the 12-minute short, *Mami Wata*. The result is a near-hypnotic film of a murky primordial soup that gets breathtakingly close to the bristly manatees. Watching the lumbering forms drift closer, one is forced to agree with zoologist Alfred Brehm when he noted: "Any animal expert who, in matters of Sirenia, is drawn to think of those mythical beings of ancient times who, half women, half fish, reside below crystalline waves of the oceans and who, with wondrous songs and still-more wondrous gestures, with a tilt of their heads and fire in their eyes, entice mortal men to come to them, to play with them, to caress them – and to perish, would be mistaken. […] One would require a truly lively imagination to see mermaids in these creatures, even if glimpsed from afar. If these plump, lethargic creatures, have anything at all in common with the beautiful female form, it is that their mammary glands are also found on the chest (between the front flippers) and protrude in a more breast-like fashion than in other mammals."[4] This brings us to another key category in developing Dirk Meinzer's world:

c) Sirens for which a "lively imagination" is, if not necessary, then certainly helpful in identifying them

Dirk Meinzer works passionately on the surface of things, where the true seduction lies in the detail. It is precisely this fetish for the superficial, so often denounced as virtually immoral in Western cultural criticism, that creates the spaces in which the observers' fantasies can be unleashed. These spaces are hardly impressive in terms of size – many of them are compact miniatures that demand viewers observe them at the most intimate proximity. Likewise, some titles reveal a love for petiteness of form, with those for works such as *Mäuslesarg* (Little Mouse Coffin), 2007 and *Männle auf Brache* (Little Man on Fallow Land), 2007 drawing on the southern German diminutive affix '-le'.

Dirk Meinzer sees surface ornamentation as much more than a mere question of secondary decorations and embellishments. As is the case with, for example, his Anatolian carpets of woven goat hair that are scattered with salacious *Micro Nudes*, Dirk Meinzer often creates tangible links to the original meaning of ornaments, to a *Rare Image of Paradise*, 2009 and to ancient female fertility symbols. In paintings and drawings he skilfully ignites the evocative power of ornamental lines and nets. In a variety of works on

Das Ornament als Oberflächenphänomen ist für Dirk Meinzer weit mehr als ein dienendes Zier- und Schmuckwerk. Oft knüpft er wie zum Beispiel im Falle der anatolischen aus Ziegenhaar gewebten, nunmehr mit anzüglichen *Micro-Nudes* gespickten Kelim-Teppiche konkret an die ursprüngliche Bedeutung von Ornamenten an, hier an eine *seltene Paradiesvorstellung*, 2009 und an eine uralte weibliche Sexual- und Fruchtbarkeitssymbolik. Dann wieder versteht er es, in Zeichnung und Malerei die starke Evokationskraft von ornamentalen Bändern und Geflechten zu aktivieren. In unterschiedlichen Arbeiten auf Papier und Leinwand, aber auch bei dem vielfachen Einsatz einer Schwarz-Weiß-Streifung, erschafft Dirk Meinzer eine Matrix, die Figur und Grund enthierarchisiert, durch optische Täuschung (scheinbar) dynamisiert und so die halluzinatorischen Sensorien der Betrachter reizt. Die Serie *Präapokalyptikum*, 2001–2007, eine Reihe infernalischer Tannenwaldbilder, ist dafür ein prägnantes Beispiel. Wer diese Bilder längere Zeit betrachtet, nimmt schwindsüchtig-vibrierende Landschaftsformationen wahr. Sie erinnern an die grellen Blitze und Punkte, die einem versehentlichen Blick in eine helle Lichtquelle folgen und dann hinter den geschlossenen Augenlidern einen wilden Tanz aufführen können. Hier ist etwas zu erfahren von der ‚Präzision im Vagen', die Dirk Meinzer selbst so benennt, und einmal mehr wird deutlich, dass der Begriff ‚Eigen-Gebung' kein schlechter Ersatz für den Begriff ‚Wahr-Nehmung' wäre.

Auch die 1999 begonnene Werkgruppe *Totalzensierte Pornohefte* führt dies je nach persönlicher Disposition der Betrachter vor Augen. Sämtliche Obszönitäten hat Dirk Meinzer mit der Mentalität eines präzise sein Messer im 90- Grad-Winkel führenden Tranchiermeisters herausgeschnitten. So werden die Zeitschriften zu Freudenheimen, in deren kubistisch-komplexes Raumprogramm sich die entblößten Verführerinnen bis in die letzten, nicht mehr einsehbaren Séparées zurückgezogen haben. Was dem Betrachter bleibt, ist einmal mehr dessen lebhafte Einbildungskraft. Und ist das Kopfkino erst beflügelt, so fügen sich auch all die anderen Arbeiten Dirk Meinzers zu einer erweiterten Schöpfungsgeschichte – fortgesetzt von einem modernen Hexenmeister, der sein Handwerk beherrscht. Was entsteht, ist eine Heerschar von

d) Hybridkreaturen

In den Materialcollagen und Assemblagen, die Dirk Meinzer unter dem Titel *Bioaktive Subjekte* zusammenfasst, und in der Gestalt der *Schreckpopanze* prallen Dinge in einer Weise aufeinander, die der legendären Begegnung von Regenschirm und Nähmaschine auf einem Seziertisch in nichts

v

paper and canvas, along with repeated use of black-and-white stripes, Dirk Meinzer creates a matrix that eliminates the hierarchies between image and background, and that stimulates the viewer's hallucinogenic senses by (seemingly) generating movement through optical illusions. The series *Preapocalypticon*, 2001–2007, with its hellish images of fir-tree forests, serves as a fitting example of this. Anyone looking at these works for an extended period begins to perceive ghastly, vibrating landscapes. They are reminiscent of the garish flashes and spots that dance a wild dance behind closed eyes after accidentally looking into a bright light. This reveals a little of what Dirk Meinzer calls "precision in obscurity" – once again, mere perception here is not enough, we have to actively construct the images of ourselves.

74–79

Totally Censored Pornos, a group of works that Dirk Meinzer began in 1999, will also be perceived differently according to the individual viewer. With the mindset of a master butcher, Dirk Meinzer guided his knife at a perfect right angle to slice out every single hint of obscenity from his material. He has thus transformed magazines into pleasure homes, where the temptresses exposed on the page have retreated to the most distant private rooms, hidden from view somewhere in the complex cubist structure of the space. We viewers are left with nothing but our own lively powers of imagination. And once our cerebral cinemas have opened their doors, all Meinzer's other works come together in an extended story of creation – a story driven by a modern-day warlock, who is truly a master of his craft. The result is a legion of

119–131

d) Hybrid creatures

In the material collages and assemblages that Dirk Meinzer calls his *Bioactive Subjects* and in his collection of *Scarecrows*, things collide in a manner that is nothing short of the legendary chance meeting on a dissecting table of a sewing machine and an umbrella. A clearly frightened *Little Bird Spirit*,

105

nachsteht. So besteht zum Beispiel der verschreckt starrende *Vögeligeist*, 2008, aus türkisschillernden Eisvogelfedern, großen Glasaugen, aus Spaghetti, die unter Buchbinderleim eine lange Nase machen, einer facettierten, grünschimmernden Hightech-Fresnelfolie, und einem kleinen schäbigen Plastiktausendfüßler, der zum Auswurf eines Kaugummiautomaten gehören dürfte. In *Hasenmond*, 2005, kommen Acryl, Aluminium und Pommes zu einer landschaftlichen Romanze zusammen – und über ihr steigt ein wunderschön seidiger Hasenfellmond auf.

In vielen der in Collagebauweise errichteten *Sirenenheime* spielen delikate Tiere und Tierfragmente, die größtenteils den Bastionen deutscher Asservatenkammern durch konzeptionelle Überschreitung bürokratischer Grenzen abgerungen sind, eine große Rolle. Nach ihrem sinnlosen, von bloßem Gewinnstreben und naivem Exotismuskult motivierten Tod drapiert Dirk Meinzer die taxidermisch zugerichteten Globalisierungsopfer geradezu festlich mit und in all dem albernen und dennoch magischen Glitter und Glanz unserer westlichen Welt: mit Lametta und Strass, mit Neonklebepunkten, Glasaugen und schrillbunten Pompons und unversehens gelingt eine wechselseitige Auratisierung der Dinge. Viele dieser Arbeiten sind zudem angetan mit phosphoreszierenden und fluoreszierenden Farben und nicht wenige sind von Vergänglichem unterfüttert: Sie bestehen im Kern aus Naturmaterialien und einst Essbarem, das durch einen Überzug aus Buchbinderleim zwar erstarrt, olfaktorisch aber längst nicht immer akkurat versiegelt ist. So entstehen groteske Gesichter und Mischwesen, die gleichermaßen von

VI

der Fülle des Lebens wie vom Tod erzählen, von Anziehung und Abstoßung, von Gier und Ekel und von ihrer jeweils engen Verwandtschaft zu Sylphen, Nixen und Nymphen, zu Melusinen und Undinen, zu Popanzen, Dämonen, Hexen und Elfen. Und wenn nach alltäglicher Zurschaustellerei eben all dieser Mischwesen die Lichtquelle, die sie in Szene setzt – zum Beispiel die von Dirk Meinzer eingesetzte, grell leuchtende historische Leuchtturm-Gürtellinse – erlischt, durchspukt noch minutenlang ein geisterhaftes Nachleuchten den stillen musealen Raum.

e) Sirenen, die aus der Ferne rufen

Dirk Meinzer ist ein ausgesprochen kenntnisreicher, aber auch spitzbübischer Ethnokult-Junkie, der seine in der Kindheit verwurzelte Schwarzwaldfaszination, mit Island, Papua-Neuguinea, China, Mexiko und vor allem mit

2008, for example, is the product of shimmering turquoise kingfisher feathers, big glass eyes, spaghetti held in place with bookbinding glue to form a nose, a faceted green-shimmering high-tech Fresnel lens and a small, shabby plastic millipede that looks as if it has just been spat out of a gumball machine. *Hare Moon*, 2005 combines acrylic, aluminium and chips to create a scenic romance beneath a divinely silky moon of hare's fur.

Graceful creatures or fragments of creatures, most of which have been wrested from the fortifications of German evidence rooms by conceptually transcending bureaucratic boundaries, play leading roles in many of the collage-like *siren homes*. Dirk Meinzer takes these taxidermied victims of globalization – their senseless deaths motivated purely by profit and a naive worship of the exotic – and drapes them almost festively with all the absurd yet magical glitz and glamour of the West: tinsel and rhinestones, neon-dot stickers, glass eyes and garish pompons. This inadvertently results in a reciprocal 'auratisation' of the things – they lend each other cultural and emotional value. Many of these works are also decked out in phosphorescent and fluorescent colours, and more than a few are padded with perishables: natural and once-edible materials under a layer of bookbinding glue that, despite setting the materials in place, does not fully withhold their olfactory character. The result is a series of grotesque faces and hybrid creatures that have as much to say about the richness of life as they do about death. They talk of attraction and repulsion, of voracity and disgust. They reveal the intimacy of their relationships with sylphs, mermaids and nymphs, with Melusines and Undines, with bogeymen, demons, witches and elves. And even when these hybrid creatures are finished for the day, and the lights – such as Dirk Meinzer's glaringly bright antique lighthouse drum lens – that focus all eyes on them fall dark, they continue to spit out into the silence of the museum their ghostly phosphorescent glow.

e) Sirens that call from afar

Dirk Meinzer is a fantastically knowledgeable, yet mischievous ethnojunkie, who has taken his childhood fascination with the Black Forest and blended it with a love of Iceland, Papua New Guinea, China, Mexico and above all Africa. *Dung Warrior*, 2007, for example, brings the exotic essence of Africa to European exhibition spaces. This work owes its existence to elephant droppings mixed with cement and decorated with aluminium and vulture down. Created on a German kitchen table, the warrior is a lasting memorial to the practice of using art to appropriate the foreign and the unknown.

20 Afrika verquickt. Aus Afrika duftet die exotische Note des *Dungkrieger*, 2007 in das europäische Ausstellungswesen herüber. Er verdankt sein Dasein den Hinterlassenschaften von Elefanten, angereichert mit Zement, verziert mit Alu und Geierflaum. Entstanden auf einem deutschen Küchentisch setzt er der Strategie einer schöpferischen Anverwandlung des Fremden und Unbekannten ein nachhaltiges Denkmal.

Dirk Meinzer beschwört das Lebendige in den Materialien und Dingen. Er greift sowohl in den Objekten als auch in performativen, teils von Klang und Musik begleiteten Handlungsformen auf Versatzstücke authentischer religiöser Praxis zu, um zwischen Alchemie, Scharlatanerie und Neo-Schamanismus hindurchlavierend der seltenen Kombination von Magie und Humor immer wieder neue, verblüffende Auftritte zu verschaffen. In einem freien schöpferischen Umgang spielt er mit Fetisch, Ritual und Kult. So wird eine Kokospalmwedelhütte zu einem Tempel für einen weißen mit den eigenen Zähnen hasengleich erknabberten, schwarzwaldbasierten

156 Schaumstoff-Tannenbaum unter tröstlichem Licht. In vielen Arbeiten wird der Mami Wata-Kult ventiliert und persifliert. Dieser erzählt von einer afrikanischen Meeresgöttin, einer hellhäutigen, fischschwänzigen Wassernixe, die als Grenzgängerin zwischen der europäischen und afrikanischen Kultur

2–15 von den Ewe, Togo, verehrt wird. Die filigranen *Sturmwinddämonen*, 2004, sind wunderschöne kleine Pretiosen, die in Kooperation mit einem tansanischen Hexenmeister in monatelanger Arbeit als Collagen aus Insekten, Insektenflügeln, Leim und Lack entstanden sind, um unversehens zu einem zarten Gruß an den Manieristen Giuseppe Arcimboldo zu werden. Wer sie genauer betrachtet, dem schauen Gesichter und Gestalten entgegen; wer das Abenteuer exotischer Küche und Naturmedizin eingehen will, der mag diese Bilder beherzt als nachvollziehbare Rezepte lesen und nutzen.

161 Auch *sympathicus boheme*, 2006, eine mehrteilige zebragestreifte Zauninstallation, die mobil und variabel verwinkelbar in jeder Ausstellungssituation von den Gästen tatsächlich ‚besessen' werden darf, scheint der afrikanischen Steppe zu entstammen: Sie definiert ein kompliziertes Hier und Dort, ein Innen und Außen, um genau dies mit dem für die Augen ermüdenden op-artistischen Verwirrspiel der Schwarz-Weiß-Streifung hinfort zu tarnen. Und: Befragt man den Zaun eindringlicher bezüglich seiner Qualitäten als *Sirenenheim*, offenbart sich überraschend dessen Wohnqualität für die im Althochdeutschen so bezeichneten Zaunreiterinnen ‚hagazussa' und damit ist statt Afrika eher der kühle Norden aufgerufen.

Vor allem Island, dessen eruptive, vulkanische Oberfläche, die die lediglich vorübergehenden Stadien aller Landschaften, Seen und Berge sichtbar

Dirk Meinzer evokes the vitality of the materials and things. In the objects and in performative acts that are at times accompanied by sounds and music, he captures fragments of authentic religious practices to traverse alchemy, charlatanism and neo-shamanism and cast the unusual combination of magic and humour in ever new, always stunning scenes. He takes a freely creative approach to playing with the notions of fetishes, rituals and cults. Thus, a hut made of coconut palm fronds becomes a comfortably lit temple for a Black-Forest-style fir tree that has gnawed itself, rabbit-like, out of a block of white foam. Many of his works reflect on and satirise the Mami Wata cult. Mami Wata is an African sea goddess, a mermaid with a fairer-than-usual complexion who is worshipped as a link between the African and European cultures of Togo's Ewe people. The delicate *Windstorm Demons*, 2004 are small, exquisite treasures that are the product of months of collaborative work with a Tanzanian warlock. These collages of insects, insect wings, glue and lacquer become a surprising, subtle salute to the Mannerist Giuseppe Arcimboldo. Anyone observing them closely will see faces and figures returning their gaze, and those wishing to embark on an adventure into exotic cuisine and natural medicine should read these images as recipes and dare to try them out at home.

Sympathetic Bohemian, 2006 – a multipart, zebra-striped, flexible fence installation that viewers can actually sit on – also appears to be a product of the African savannah. It defines a complex here and now, an inside and out, and then disguises precisely these elements by exhausting the eye through the op-art confusion of the black-and-white stripes. What is more, if one examines the fence more closely to determine its qualities as a *siren home,* it reveals, quite astonishingly, that it is the perfect residence for the 'fence spirits' known in Old High German as 'hagazussa'. Rather than invoking Africa, this piece speaks of colder northern climes.

Iceland, with its eruptive, volcanic surface that exposes the temporary nature of every landscape, lake and mountain, has had a particularly lasting effect on Dirk Meinzer. His travels have taken him there on a number of occasions and it was there that he traced the footsteps of Dieter Roth. It is likely that this provided the driving force behind his increasing artistic exploration of process of decay in all its guises. As a result, his work includes

VII

macht, hat Dirk Meinzer nachhaltig beeinflusst. Mehrfach führten ihn Reisen nach Island. Dort hat er sich auf den Spuren Dieter Roths bewegt und dies mag eine forcierte künstlerische Auseinandersetzung mit Verfallsprozessen jeglicher Art bewirkt haben. Somit finden sich in seinem Werk

f) Erscheinungen, die sich der Ewigkeit verweigern

Jeder weiß, dass Badezimmerfugen und Kühlschrankecken im Zuge selbstorganisierter Schimmelkultur plötzlich und unerwartet zu ‚Sirenenheimen' werden können. Schädliches, oft sogar Pathogenes, aber eben auch eine verblüffende Schönheit und Pracht können erblühen. Schimmel kann ausgesprochen nützlich, ja sogar heilsam sein. Ganz gleich jedoch wie und wo er auftritt, immer schafft er das wehmütige Bild eines unausweichlichen Zugleich von Leben und Tod. Genau dieser janusköpfige Zug reizt Dirk Meinzer und so setzt er sich seit Ende der 1990er Jahre obsessiv mit allen erdenklichen Erscheinungsformen von Schimmelpilzen auseinander. Er konsultiert Experten, studiert Literatur und experimentiert in Laboren gemeinsam mit Mikrobiologen und Chemikern. 1999 kulminiert zum Beispiel eine derart intensive Auseinandersetzung in der Arbeit *Schimmelschimmel*, die aus 2116 quadratischen, unterschiedlich beimpften Petrischalen bestand und nach genauer Berechnung an einem vorbestimmten Tag als großes zusammengesetztes Bild einen ungestüm in der Landschaft aufsteigenden Schimmel zur Erscheinung brachte.

Was Dirk Meinzer erforscht, ist die im konkreten und übertragenen Sinne vorhandene Kulturfähigkeit und Bildmacht von Schimmel und dabei natürlich konsequent folgernd die Frage der künstlerischen Delegation in diesen Bereich. Die 2003 entstandenen C-Prints mit dem Titel *Rhizomorphe Landschaften* gehen zum Beispiel auf Prozesse zurück, die in Petrischalen gebettete, durchaus ansehnliche Großbilddias über sich ergehen lassen mussten. Phantastische Neverlands entstehen. *Megaron*, 2009, ist ein im Ausstellungsraum beobachtbarer Feldversuch. Anfangs knackig-grüne Salatgurken gehen in ihrem Latexbett den Weg des Vergänglichen. Zu verfolgen ist die Eigendynamik eines Prozesses, die vor allem durch die gegebenen Lichtverhältnisse, die Temperatur und Luftfeuchtigkeit beeinflusst wird. Folglich wabert über Wochen hinweg eine museal wenig vertraute süßliche Duftwolke durch die Luft und das sich täglich neu einstellende schwindsüchtige Bild kann mal einem lieblich-fliederfarbenen Gärtchen, mal einer braunen Obszönitätenzucht gleichen.

Immer ist der Zufall bei diesen schimmelbasierten Arbeiten ein verlässlicher Partner. Ihm bietet sich je nach örtlicher Gegebenheit allerlei Gekrabbel,

f) Manifestations that reject eternity

Everyone knows that self-organising mildew colonies can suddenly and unexpectedly turn bathroom cracks and fridge corners into siren homes. These colonies can be harmful, even pathogenic, but they can also blossom into displays of startling beauty. Mildew can be extremely useful and can even have healing qualities. Regardless of how and where it appears it inevitably paints a melancholy picture of an inescapable simultaneity of life and death. It is precisely this Janus-faced force that appeals to Dirk Meinzer and has driven his passion for working with all manifestations of mildew since the end of the 1990s. He consults experts, studies literature and works with microbiologists and chemists to conduct laboratory experiments. In 1999, for example, one such intensive project culminated in the work *Schimmelschimmel* (Mildewmildew). In German, the word *Schimmel* can mean both 'mildew' and 'a white horse'. The work was made of 2.116 square petri dishes inoculated with different microorganisms. Dirk Meinzer made a series of precise calculations to ensure that the cultures flourished on a predetermined day to reveal a large white horse rearing dramatically in the foreground.

VIII

The focus of Dirk Meinzer's research is the literal and figurative cultivability and visual power of mildew, and of course the consistent analysis of the function of art in this area. For example, his C-prints from 2003 entitled *Rhizomorph Landscapes* are the result of subjecting perfectly fine large-format transparencies to a variety of processes in petri dishes. The end products are a series of images of fantastical Neverlands. *Megaron*, 2009 is a field study that can be observed in the exhibition space. What start out as crunchy green cucumbers gradually go the way of all things perishable in their latex beds. The work displays the unique dynamics of the process, on which the preset lighting, temperature and humidity have a defining influence. The result is a mawkish scent, entirely foreign in a museum context, that wafts through the air week after week. This is accompanied by an image of destruction that changes by the day and can resemble anything from a charming little lilac garden to a brown breeding ground of obscenities.

Coincidence is invariably a reliable contributor to these mildew-based works. Depending on the local conditions, any number of hard-working creepy-crawlies, worms and other creatures offer their services to coincidence – and thus, from destruction and decay, a work of art emerges.

Gewürm und Getier als fleißiger Mitarbeiterstab an – und so entsteht durch Zerstörung und Verfall ein Werk.

g) Lächler

Wer sich fremd fühlt, wer gar Feindschaft zu spüren meint, der setzt meist unwillkürlich das sprichwörtlich entwaffnende Lächeln auf. Vornehmlich ist das Duchenne'sche Lächeln anzuraten, jenes Lächeln, bei dem die Augen mitspielen und somit die Aufrichtigkeit des Signals bekunden.

Dirk Meinzer hat seit 2004 als spezielle Abteilung seiner Wunderkammer eine ganze Ahnengalerie von so genannten *Lächlern* geschaffen: In primitivistischer Flachheit sind sämtliche Exemplare stets frontal innerhalb eines engen Bildausschnitts zu sehen. Ist die Familienzugehörigkeit unübersehbar, so sind jedoch die Dargestellten jeweils sehr eigen. Mit den standardisierten Symbol-Smileys der zeitgenössischen Medienwelt oder den überanstrengten Berufslächlern der Servicebranchen haben sie wenig zu tun. Vielleicht ist eher das so genannte archaische Lächeln eine hilfreiche Referenz.

Manche wie zum Beispiel der *Modder-Lächler*, 2008, haben dabei eine klar konturierte Präsenz. Andere wie *Punktegeist*, 2007 sind kaum auszumachen; sie zeigen sich dem Betrachter als instabile Epiphanien. Einige sind über den Titel als Portrait geoutet: So verweist *Lächler argante II*, 2007 auf eine keltische Hexe; ein anderer ist das Portrait des kommunistischen Revolutionärs *Colonel Fabien*, 2007. Mitunter fühlt sich der Betrachter wie der Kommissar, der an den Fundort einer (Wasser)leiche zitiert wurde, oder eben wie der Kunsthistoriker, der schon bei Jean Dubuffet in den Flecken und Krusten von Gemälden und Materialcollagen die Identifizierbarkeit von u.a. Henri Michaux, Antonin Artaud oder Jean Fautrier zu bestätigen hatte.

IX

Damit ist ausgesprochen, dass Dirk Meinzers *Lächler* nicht etwa, wie der Titel der Werkgruppe glauben machen könnte, durchweg liebenswerte Gesellen sind. Manch einer kündet sogar mit weit aufgerissenen Augen von einem beunruhigenden Zustand der Hysterie oder Verzückung. „Nicht die Schönheit und Lieblichkeit ist unsere Stärke, unsere Kraft ist eher das Gegenteil, die Hässlichkeit, dämonische Leidenschaft und die groteske Genialität der Größe, vor allem aber der Humor mit seinem Heer von originellen Gestalten"[5], ist bei Ernst Barlach zu lesen.

So erscheinen einige der Meinzer'schen *Lächler* etwas dümmlich. Mal scheinen sie trunken, mal sardonisch, spöttisch oder höhnisch zu grinsen. Manche schneiden infantile Fratzen, andere lachen breit und zeigen dabei

g) Smilers

Anyone who feels out of place, anyone who senses even a hint of hostility, will instinctively break into what has long been described as the proverbially disarming smile. A particularly good choice in such a situation is the Duchenne smile, which involves the eyes as well as the mouth and thereby signals the sincerity of the expression.

Since 2004, Dirk Meinzer has dedicated a special area of his cabinet of curiosities to an ancestral gallery of *Smilers*. Each smiler is depicted head-on, in simple two-dimensionality and filling most of the space around it. Although the family ties are unmistakable, each image is distinct in itself. They have little in common with the standardised smiley icons of today's media world or with the forced professional smiles of the service industry. Perhaps the classic Archaic smile provides a more fitting comparison.

Some of them, such as *Sludge Smiler*, 2008, have a clearly defined presence. Others, such as *Speckled Spirit*, 2007, are almost impossible to make out and seem to the viewer to be merely capricious apparitions. A few have titles that reveal them as portraits: *Argante Smiler II*, 2007 was inspired by a Celtic witch, while *Colonel Fabien*, 2007 depicts the communist revolutionary. Surrounded by these images, the viewer can feel like a police superintendent called to the scene of where a body has been found (perhaps in the water), or like an art historian charged with confirming the likenesses of Henri Michaux, Antonin Artaud, Jean Fautrier et al. in the spots and incrustations of Jean Dubuffet's paintings and material collages.

49
54
44
51

This indicates that Dirk Meinzers smilers are not, as their name suggests, always likeable fellows. Some of them, with their wildly staring eyes, even seem to be unsettlingly hysterical or delirious. As Ernst Barlach said, "Our strength does not lie in beauty or charm; rather, our power lies on the other side, in ugliness, demonic passion, the grotesque brilliance of size, and, more than anything, in all the ingenious guises of humour."⁵

X

Some of Dirk Meinzer's smilers therefore appear somewhat foolish. They grin drunkenly, mockingly, sneeringly or tauntingly. Some pull immature faces while others smile broadly and – as the only mammal here – accompany a rather positive disposition with bared teeth. It is clear that exploring the animal kingdom will prove helpful in describing these cases – Dirk Meinzer himself has chosen titles that reveal inspiration in the shape of frogs and pigs.

– als einziges Säugetier – begleitend zu einer tendenziell positiven Gemütslage ihre Zähne. Dass Ausflüge ins Tierreich vor allem in diesen Fällen zur Beschreibungshilfe werden, ist nahe liegend. Frosch und Schwein zitiert Dirk Meinzer via Titel selbst herbei.

h) die, die direkt ins Blut gehen

Als moderner Hexenmeister hat Dirk Meinzer – angetan in einem passgenau gehäkelten Zebrastreifenkostüm mit Tanzpenis – einen besonders eindrucksvollen Auftritt in seinem *Tabulabor*, 2004, in einer abenteuerlich blubbernden und dampfenden Destilleninstallation. Unversehens steigen dann auf Saisonobst basierende Alkoholdünste in die Nasen der eigentlich auf reinen Augenschmaus gepolten Kunstkonsumenten. Wer der Versuchung sogar faktisch erliegt und den Fusel probiert, dem freilich diffundieren die Sirenen direkt ins Blut. Werden auf diese Weise diverse transgressive Stadien erprobt, lacht sich Dirk Meinzer schelmisch hinweg – um dabei schenkelklopfend einzustimmen in ein längst historisches Gelächter, das die Fluxus-Künstler aber auch die Surrealisten und Dadaisten entfacht haben. Und mit Blick auf die Arbeiten Dirk Meinzers meint man Max Ernst herauszuhören: „Wenn die Vernunft schläft, singen die Sirenen."[6]

1 Dirk Meinzer in einer E-mail an die Verfasserin vom 11.1.2009.
2 Jorge Luis Borges, *Die Analytische Sprache John Wilkins'*.
   In: ders. *Das Eine und die Vielen. Essays zur Literatur*, München 1966, S. 212.
3 Michel Foucault, *Die Ordnung der Dinge*, Frankfurt am Main 1974, S. 17
   (Erstausgabe: *Les mots et les choses*, 1966).
4 Alfred Brehm, *Brehms Tierleben*. In: ders. *Allgemeine Kunde des Tierreichs. Säugetiere – Dritter Band*, Leipzig und Wien 1891, S.553.
5 Dross Friedrich (Hg.), *Ernst Barlach. Die Briefe 1888–1924, Bd.1*, München 1968, S. 233.
6 Vgl. XI

I Sirene, um 550 v. Chr., Marmor, Ny Carlsberg Glyptotek, Kopenhagen.
   In: Ernst Buschor, *Die Musen des Jenseits,* München 1944, S.41.
II Odysseus und die Sirenen, Rotfiguriger Mischkrug, um 480 v. Chr. In: Ebd.
III Stellersche Seekuh. In: Reverend H. N. Hutchinson, *Extinct Monsters; a Popular Account of Some of the Larger Forms of Ancient Animal Life*, New York 1893.
IV Schnauze einer Seekuh. In: Erna Mohr, *Sirenen oder Seekühe*, Wittenberg 1957.
V Vogeldämon aus Syrakus, um 650 v. Chr.
   In: Ernst Buschor, *Die Musen des Jenseits,* München 1944, S.21.
VI Ausgestopfte Seekuh. Postkarte aus der Sammlung von Holger Steen.
VII Giuseppe Arcimboldo, *Das Wasser*, 1566, Öl auf Erlenholz, 66,5 × 50,5 cm, Kunsthistorisches Museum Wien.
VIII Vogeldämon, um 600 v. Chr.
   In: Ernst Buschor, *Die Musen des Jenseits,* München 1944, S.23.
IX Jean Dubuffet, *Dhôtel nuancé d'abricot*, 1947, Öl auf Leinwand, 116 × 89 cm, Centre Georges Pompidou, Paris.
X Leonardo da Vinci, *Mona Lisa*, 1503–1505, Öl auf Pappelholz, 76,8 × 53 cm, Musée du Louvre, Paris.
XI Max Ernst, *Wenn die Vernunft schläft, singen die Sirenen*, 1960, Öl auf Leinwand, 65 × 54 cm, Bayrische Staatsgemäldesammlungen. Pinakothek der Moderne, München.

h) Ones that get straight into the bloodstream

As a modern-day warlock, Dirk Meinzer – sporting a perfectly fitted, crocheted zebra costume complete with artificial penis – cuts a particularly striking figure in his *Taboo Laboratory,* 2004, which is a fascinating, bubbling, steaming distillery installation. Viewers geared towards consuming nothing but artistic eye candy are suddenly confronted with the smell of seasonal fruit-based alcohol. Anyone who actually succumbs to the temptation and tries the hooch will invariably release sirens into their bloodstream. If this results in an exploration of various stages of transcendence, Dirk Meinzer laughs away mischievously – and in doing so, he joins in heartily with the now-historic guffaws that were first sparked by the Fluxus artists, the Surrealists and the Dadaists. And looking at Dirk Meinzer's work, one can almost hear Max Ernst saying, "When reason sleeps, the sirens sing."⁶

158

XI

1   Dirk Meinzer in an e-mail to the author, 11 January 2009.
2   Jorge Luis Borges, *Die Analytische Sprache John Wilkins'.*
    In: id. *Das Eine und die Vielen. Essays zur Literatur*, Munich, 1966, p. 212.
3   Michel Foucault, *Die Ordnung der Dinge*, Frankfurt am Main, 1974, p. 17
    (original edition: *Les mots et les choses*, 1966).
4   Alfred Brehm, *Brehms Tierleben*. In: id. *Allgemeine Kunde des Tierreichs.*
    Säugetiere, – Dritter Band, Leipzig and Vienna, 1891, p. 553.
5   Dross Friedrich (Ed.), *Ernst Barlach, Die Briefe 1888-1924, Bd.1*, Munich, 1968, p. 233.
6   cp. XI

I   Siren, around 550 BC, marble, Ny Carlsberg Glyptotek, Copenhagen.
     In: Ernst Buschor, *Die Musen des Jenseits,* Munich 1944, p.41.
II   Ulysses and the Sirens, Amphora, around 480 BC. Ibid.
III Drawing of Steller's sea cow. In: Reverend H. N. Hutchinson, *Extinct Monsters;*
     a Popular Account of Some of the Larger Forms of Ancient Animal Life, New York 1893.
IV   Mouth of a sea cow. In: Erna Mohr, *Sirenen oder Seekühe,* Wittenberg 1957.
V   Bird demon from Syracuse, around 650 BC.
     In: Ernst Buschor, *Die Musen des Jenseits,* Munich 1944, p.21.
VI   Mounted sea cow. Postcard from the collection of Holger Steen.
VII Giuseppe Arcimboldo, *Water*, 1566, oil on wood, 66,5 × 50,5 cm,
     Kunsthistorisches Museum Wien, Vienna.
VIII Bird demon, around 600 BC. Ernst Buschor, *Die Musen des Jenseits,* Munich 1944, p.23.
IX   Jean Dubuffet, *Dhôtel nuancé d'abricot*, 1947, oil on canvas, 116 × 89 cm,
     Centre Georges Pompidou, Paris.
X   Leonardo da Vinci, *Mona Lisa*, 1503 – 1505, oil on cottonwood, 76,8 × 53 cm,
     Musée du Louvre, Paris.
XI   Max Ernst, *When reason sleeps, the sirens sing*, 1960, oil on canvas, 65 × 54 cm,
     Bayrische Staatsgemäldesammlungen. Pinakothek der Moderne, Munich.

Andrea Tippel
Liebreiz

Darwin hat das Wort ‚win' in seinem englischen Namen, nomen est omen (und ‚rad').

Seine *Entstehung der Arten* wird immer noch als eine der drei größten Kränkungen der Menschheit gehandelt. (Kopernikus und Freud sind die beiden anderen Bösewichte.)

Dirk Meinzer wagt sich weit in die Sinnlichkeit dieser Übergangssphären vor, in die des Unter- und des Aufgangs in ihnen, des Herüben und Hinüben, und in die sie begleitenden Empfindungen. Das geht nicht mehr mit Worten, sonst gäbe es diesen Diskurs nicht. Also wird hier von Bildern geredet – ouroboros.

Die Ahnengalerie der Lächler schlägt einen anderen, einen Nebenweg der Ahnenforschung, den unvergleichlich viel längeren und breiteren darwinschen, ein, der weit bis vor die Prähistorie zurückreicht, nicht mehr fassbar, aber die Ahnung unwiderstehlich heraufbeschwörend. Die Ahnung ist das starke Undeutliche und doch Gewisse im Innern, und sie ist die von Bedeutung, die hochgeschätzte.

Wir folgen ihr. Von so was spricht Agnes Martin, wenn sie den Begriff Vollkommenheit (perfection) jongliert.

Es gibt nicht nur Einheit noch nur Plötzlichkeit, aber Plötzlichkeit in der Einheit und ganz bestimmt Einheit in der Plötzlichkeit, und es gibt das Verschwimmen, die Übergänge zwischen Tier und Mensch. Nichts könnte abgründiger sein.

Seelisch sind evolutionäre Prozesse nie abgeschlossen, also auch ikonisch nicht, und evolutionär können Menschen nur zurückschauen, vor ihnen liegt Fiktion. Aber die Tiere können (ihre) Zukunft in uns sehen.

In den Lächlern ist das menschliche Gesichtsschema, das Vis-à-vis, auf das wir anspringen, oft gerade noch erkennbar in der Auflösung der Details und der Konsistenz, und besonders der Blick changiert in alle Richtungen und zieht sich bis ans Ende des Tunnels der Zeit so weit zurück wie der Blick des Tiers sich vor dem unseren. Das Augenpaar bricht vielfach auseinander, und die Augen wandern wieder an beide Seiten des Kopfes, dorthin zurück, wo sie einst waren.

Tiere formen schon Menschen und Menschen noch Tiere. Oder formen sich Tiere Menschen, den Künstler, so, wie sich Menschen Tiere formen, um (sie) zu sein?

Andrea Tippel
Charm

Translation by R. M. Goddard

Darwin has got the word 'win' in his name: nomen est omen (and 'rad').

His *Origin of Species* is still traded as one of the three greatest insults to humanity. (Copernicus and Freud are the other two villains).

Dirk Meinzer dares to go deep into the sensuality of these spheres of transition, into their decline and their emergence, into the hither and thither, and into the feelings accompanying them. That is no longer possible with words, otherwise there wouldn't be this discourse. Here then, pictures are spoken of – ouroboros.

The ancestral portrait gallery of The Smilers follows another path, a genealogical byway, the incomparably far longer and broader Darwinian one, which reaches far back to before prehistory and is no longer comprehensible, but is one which irresistibly evokes the presentiment. The presentiment is powerfully vague, and yet certain within and it is that of meaning, the revered. We follow it. Agnes Martin speaks of this when she juggles with the concept of perfection.

There is not mere unity or mere suddenness but suddenness in unity and certainly unity in suddenness and there are the indistinctness and the transitions between animal and human. Nothing could be more abysmal.

Psychically, evolutionary processes are never completed and therefore neither are they iconically. In evolutionary terms, humans can only look backwards, ahead of them lies fiction. But animals can see (their) future in us.

In those smiling, the human facial pattern, the vis-à-vis at which we start, is often just discernible in the resolution of details and consistency. In particular, the regard changes in all directions and withdraws to the end of the tunnel of time, as far back as the regard of an animal recoils from ours. The pair of eyes multiply breaks apart and the eyes migrate back to either side of the head, back to where they once were.

Animals already form humans and humans still form animals. Or is it that animals form humans, the artist, just as humans form animals to be (them)?

"There is no way to decide if the tamer trained the lion to jump after he cracks his whip or if the lion trained the tamer to crack his whip before he jumps !" (Tomas Schmit). Alienation and embrace lie first in similarity.

"Can a being see something without being it or at least becoming it or becoming less?" (Dieter Roth).

To look deeply there requires a brave gaze of kinship with and reconcili-

„There is no way to decide if the tamer trained the lion to jump after he cracks his whip or if the lion trained the tamer to crack his whip before he jumps!" (Tomas Schmit). Erst im Ähnlichen liegen Befremdung und Umarmung.

„Kann ein Wesen etwas sehen, ohne das zu sein oder wenigstens zu werden oder weniger zu werden?" (Dieter Roth).

Da hineinzuschauen verlangt den mutigen Blick des Verschwisterns und Versöhnens in den unheimlich offenen Raum, den der Abschied von Mensch und Tier geschaffen hat, das Zwischenspiel vom Ich zum Du zum Wir und wieder zurück während der gemeinsamen Zeit. Organische gleich sichtbare und seelische gleich empathische, sich identifizierende lebendige Transmutation (identitas: welch ein herüber- und hinüberschillernder Begriff, wie geschaffen für Meinzers Bilder).

Er hat ihn, den wilden ahnungsvollen Blick in dieses Niemandsland, das gleich an unsere Gefilde stößt, diesen scheinbar unüberbrückbaren Abgrund, kann dahinein und darin sehen und auch noch uns Bilder davon zeigen. Die Welt der Abbildungen aber ist eine andere als die seine, und Tiere tragen keinen Schmuck im menschlichen Sinn. Sie sind von blanker Schönheit. Dirk der Lächler.

Die Tiere befolgen das ikonoklastische Gebot ganz. Wie viel Vogelschiss klebte an der Jüdischen Braut, hängte sie an einer Tankstelle. Schrieben die Bienen hier oder der Laubenvogel, sie schrieben vermutlich dasselbe, aber über uns.

Die ikonische Indolenz der Tiere, (und doch hätte Zeuxis, dank der getäuschten Vögel, beinahe den Wettbewerb in der Malerei gewonnen, aber er unterlag der Fähigkeit, den Menschen täuschen zu können) die Ikonolatrie des Menschen, sie sind Unterstellungen von den jeweils anderen Ufern über das große Dunkel hinweg, Vermutungen. Was steht auf den Steinen, den Muscheln? Wie liegen die Blätter, stehen die Pilze? Grammatik? Information? Und warum sollte das nicht auch für den Schiss gelten? Unlesbare Spuren von Ritualen?

Diese Übergänge sind für uns die schwierigsten, das kann man sehen an den niemals endenden Crossover-Metamorphosen im Wiesen- und Höllengrund aller kulturellen Ikonik.

Dirk Meinzer ist da unterwegs, und es ist ihm dort oft selbst unheimlich, aber es verlockt ihn zutiefst, und unbändig rauschhaft, also erträgt er's, mit Wonne.

Das Theriomorphe und Theriopneumische des Menschen und das Anthropomorphe und Anthropopneumische des Tiers, diese brisanten

ation to the uncanny open space which created the departure of man and animal, the interlude from I to you to we and back again during the common time. The organic as the visible and the psychic as the empathetic, living transmutation, identifying with itself (identitas: how the concept fluoresces back and forth, as though created expressly for Meinzer's pictures).

He has it, the wild foreboding regard into this no-mans-land abutting our realm, this apparently unbridgeable abyss. He can look into it and see in there and even show us images of it. The world of illustrations is, however, not his world; animals wear no jewellery in the human sense. They possess naked beauty. Dirk the Smiler.

Animals follow the iconoclastic command entirely. How much bird shit would stick to The Jewish Bride if she hung at a petrol station? If the bees or the bower bird were to write here, presumably they would write the same, but about us.

The iconic indolence of animals (Zeuxis almost won the painting competition thanks to the deceived birds, but he lacked the ability to deceive men) and the iconolatry of men are both assumptions from the respective opposite bank across the great darkness, presumptions. What is written on the stones, the mussels? How do the leaves lie and the mushrooms stand? Grammar? Information? And why should not this apply to the shit, too? Illegible traces of rituals?

These transitions are the most difficult for us. This can be seen from the never-ending crossover-metamorphoses in the heaven- and hell-scapes of every culture's iconography.

Dirk Meinzer is abroad there and often finds it uncanny himself, yet it entices him profoundly and intoxicates him overwhelmingly and so he can endure it, blissfully.

The theriomorph and theriopneuma essence of the human and the anthropomorph and anthropneuma essence of the animal, these explosive potentials – how do we arrive there, in between, if we really want to, as he does?

Spheres of pure paradox: self-referential, contradictory, circular – groundless. The enduring, the continually circling durance in this region so alien and yet so genuine to us, which language can already no longer illuminate after the endless time of the absence of the animal as being in, not only for or even because of us humans, unutterable; no words reach into this abyss of profound longing for a possibility of communicating with one another (?) or reach beyond this abyss.

Places without final truths. Or the place of final truth?

People are the progeny of animals. Let us ask our parents.

Potenziale – wie gelangen wir dahin, dazwischen, wenn wir es denn wollen, wie er?

Sphären reiner Paradoxie: selbstbezogen, widersprüchlich, zirkelhaft – bodenlos. Das Haftende, die immer und immer im Kreis gehende Haft in diesem uns so wildfremden und doch genuinen Gebiet, das die Sprache nach der endlosen Zeit der Absenz des Tiers als Wesen in, nicht nur für oder gar wegen uns Menschen schon nicht mehr ausleuchten kann, unsagbar, keine Wörter reichen in diesen Abgrund der tiefen Sehnsucht nach einer Möglichkeit, einander (?) zu verständigen, oder über diesen Abgrund hinweg.

Orte ohne letzte Wahrheiten. Oder Ort der letzten Wahrheit?

Menschen sind der Tiere Nachkommen. Fragen wir unsere Eltern.

Tiere können nicht monströs sein, das ist Menschenflitterkram: Ach mein schönes Äffchen, mein Bärchen, mein Häschen, mein Mäuschen. An solchen Stellen, Liebe oder Kinder, geht es wieder: Alle sollen glücklich sein, alle. Und was darin steckt, abgründige Wahrheit in diesem süßen Irrtum, das zeigt Dirk Meinzer.

Wie Menschen hier mit Tieren leben, das ist Gebrauch oder Plüsch – aber im ausgestopften Präparat liegt schon der Abgrund. Ein umwerfender Blick, dem muss man erst mal standhalten.

Zwischen Abbildung, Nachbildung, Asservat (wie Meinzer seine Tierpräparate nennt, ein Terminus aus der Kriminalistik wohlgemerkt) und Wesen liegen die nebligen Felder von Gefügigkeit und Flucht, von Annäherung und Abwenden, von Bewunderung, Dienen und Töten.

Die Präparate sind der in Form gebliebene erste Tod. Diesen Zustand können die auf einer anderen Ebene wiederbelebenden Abbildungen und Nachbildungen nicht erreichen. Der erste Tod ist per se nicht Kunst, aber im anderen kann er es sein.

Die Schönheit der Wesen ist abgründig, wir alle werden unwiderstehlich hineingesogen, und sie ist, ganz objektiv, völlig subjektiv. Schönheit ist Einsicht, Sehnsucht und Wiedererkennen, vielleicht sich.

Davor und danach ist Schönheit Akklamation, ein unerheblicher Allgemeinplatz. Und Schönheit ist die eigene Verpflichtung.

Es tut weh, einen Gorilla im Frankfurter Zoo (Charly) oder eine Katze in der Schweiz (Stummi) zu lieben, manche kennen das. Nicht mal das alte Volkslied von den zwei Königskindern kann dieses Gefühl des Schmerzes heraufbeschwören. Es geht tiefer und ist kürzer, ein Dolch. Es geht tiefer, weil sein Anfang schon am Anfang ist und nicht an irgendeinem Ende von Erfüllung, es ist nur Schmerz und keine Seligkeit.

Animals cannot be monstrous, that is human frippery: oh my pretty monkey my little bear my bunny my mousie. In such situations, with love or children it goes on: all should be happy, all. And Dirk Meinzer shows what lies therein, the abysmal truth in this sweet error.

How humans live here with animals is a matter of use or plush – but the abyss already lies within the stuffed specimen. One must first withstand a devastating look.

Between illustration, simulation, the exhibit (as Meinzer calls his animal specimens – a forensic term, it should be noted) and being lie the foggy fields of tractability and flight, of approach and avoidance, of admiration, service and killing.

The exhibits are the first death remaining in form. The illustrations and simulations which revivify on another level cannot attain this condition. The first death is per se not art, but it can be in others.

The beauty of the being is abysmal, we are all irresistibly sucked in and it is quite objectively entirely subjective. Beauty is insight, longing and recognition, perhaps oneself.

Before and after this, beauty is acclamation, an insubstantial general place. And beauty is personal duty.

It hurts to love a gorilla (Charly) in Frankfurt zoo or a cat (Stummi) in Switzerland, some people know this. Not even the old folk song about the two royal children can evoke this feeling of pain. It goes deeper and is shorter, a dagger. It goes deeper because its beginning is already at the beginning and not at some end of fulfilment, it is merely pain and not bliss.

Words can pass the lips but they remain pitiable, do not arrive, swallow themselves.

There is another way and Meinzer tells of it with his works.

Whoever penetrates so far into this furrow that it becomes an abyss once more is also very close to plants. Why is this dry fibre scaffold of a Spanish opuntia a seal and a boar?

To an ant, our furrow is no longer an abyss and to us still not one.

The jay immediately flies off when I approach and the tit when he approaches. So we appropriate them as beautiful because we cannot appropriate their love or give them ours.

The eyes migrated forwards and created the frontal pair of eyes; the astonishment of these ancestors over us and the wild dread of the animal before it. How many regards lie in one single regard?

The holy horror in the Darwinian transition, the devotion, the application, and the expansiveness of the Cartesian madness of radical exclusion,

Worte können über die Lippen gehen, aber sie bleiben elend, erreichen nicht, verschlucken sich selbst.

Es geht anders, davon spricht Meinzer mit seinen Werken.

Wer so weit eindringt in diese Furche, dass sie wieder zum Abgrund wird, der ist ganz nahe auch bei den Pflanzen. Warum ist dieses trockene Fasergerüst einer spanischen Opuntie Robbe und Eber?

Für eine Ameise ist unsere Furche kein Abgrund mehr und für uns noch keiner.

Der Eichelhäher fliegt sofort weg, wenn ich komme, und die Meise, wenn er kommt. Also eignen wir sie uns als Schönheit an, wo wir uns ihre Liebe nicht aneignen können und ihnen unsere nicht geben.

Die Augen wanderten nach vorne und schufen das frontale Augenpaar, das Erstaunen dieser Ahnen über uns und die wilde Scheu der Tiere vor ihm. Wie viele Blicke liegen in einem einzigen Blick?

Der heilige Schauder in der Darwin'schen Übergabe, die Hingabe, der Antrag, und das Expansive des Descarte'schen Wahnsinns der radikalen Exklusion, das Verbrechen, rauschen ineinander und gären in diesem abgrundseelischen Raum aus dem Moiré verdorbenen Kaviars in Kilodosen und Eisbären mit weißen Eiern bekränzt.

Vor dem Furor sind wir Menschen, und nach dem Furor sind wir wieder Menschen.

Wenn man die Menschheitsgeschichte zusammenschnurren lässt, dann stehen wir vor den industriell geschlachteten Göttern, und vor dem Entsetzen vor dieser Tat verschließen wir fest unser vorwärts gerichtetes Augenpaar.

So wie Fechner die Seele der Pflanzen durch die der Tiere, der uns Vertrauteren, aufdeckt, um uns das Unerhörte nahe zu bringen, so gibt es in Meinzers Bildern das allgegenwärtige Gesicht, bis zum Schema ganz kurz vor seinem Entschwinden, sein erneutes Hervorschwimmen und Wieder-Vergehen vor unserem verwirrten Blick.

So vieles wird unkenntlich und geht so verloren unter dem Schirm der Gewohnheit. (Denn Sophia wurde wegen ihrer ungezügelten Neugier, ihrer Tolma, schwerstens bestraft und dann doch vom gnostischen Gott rehabilitiert.)

Weil wir nicht wach im Dunkeln sein wollen, weil wir sehen wollen, um zu handeln und unserer visuellen Neugier zu frönen und unsere Augen sich ans Feuer gewöhnt haben, beleuchten wir, wenn die Dunkelheit kommt, die Bilder, die Gegenstände und Räume und löschen so die Gestirne und Erzählungen, nehmen das Funkeln der Augen der Nacht an uns.

the crime, rush together and ferment in this abyss-minded space from the moiré of rotting caviar in kilogram tins and polar bears garlanded with white eggs.

Before the furore we are humans and after the furore we are humans once more.

If one laces together human history, we stand before the industrially butchered gods and before the horror at this act we seal up our forwards-facing pair of eyes.

Just as Fechner discovers the soul of plants through that of animals, more familiar to us, in order to acquaint us with the unheard-of, there is in Meinzer's pictures the ubiquitous face, up to the schema just before its vanishing, its re-emergence and passing once again before our bewildered regard.

So much grows unrecognisable and gets so lost beneath the shield of custom. (Since Sophia was severely punished for her unbridled curiosity (tolma), only to be rehabilitated by the god of the Gnostics).

Since we do not wish to be awake in the darkness, since we wish to see in order to act and to indulge our visual curiosity and since our eyes have become accustomed to fire, we illuminate pictures, objects and spaces when the darkness comes, extinguishing the heavenly bodies and narratives, drawing down the sparkling of the eyes of night.

Lichtenberg wrote that he thought differently about something lying down or standing. How different must thinking then be by day and night?

When night falls then many of Meinzer's works glow in unfathomable difference in the same, offering us other strata of their multi-layered essence and thus giving themselves up to the night in alien rejoicing and solemnity. They show how people here live under the condition of light although half the time it is night to them. Let us first dismay ourselves and shudder in their sudden eeriness, then stretch our all too brief twilight, into which peace and leisure return as a unifying fluidum against the might of darkness, their inactivity and their dangerous blindness with open eyes; until they submerge into it.

Out of these opaque, uncanny interstices to which we give nothing more than merely our struggle against them (meanwhile, we come to learn the consequences), Dirk Meinzer the messenger brings us his colourful, intoxicating reports from the acute and frontal challenge of our own, through our own immersed essence, which he encounters there.

Lichtenberg schrieb, dass er im Liegen anders über eine Sache denke als im Stehen. Wie anders erst bei Tag und bei Nacht.

Wenn die Nacht kommt, dann erglühen viele von Meinzers Werken in der unauslotbaren Verschiedenheit im Selben, halten uns andere Schichten ihres vielschichtigen Wesens entgegen und geben sich so ihr, der Nacht, fremd, festlich und feierlich hin. Wie hiesige Menschen unter der Bedingung des Lichts leben, obwohl die halbe Zeit ihnen Nacht ist, das zeigen sie. Lassen uns erst in ihrer plötzlichen Gespenstigkeit erschrecken und schaudern und dehnen dann unsere zu kurzen Dämmerungen, in die der Friede und die Muße einkehren als vereinigendes Fluidum gegen die Macht der Dunkelheit, ihre Tatenlosigkeit und ihre gefährliche Blindheit bei geöffneten Augen; bis sie darin versinken.

Aus diesen opaken, unheimlichen Zwischenräumen, denen wir nichts mehr geben als nur unseren Kampf gegen sie (wir lernen inzwischen die Folgen kennen), bringt der Bote Dirk Meinzer uns seine bunten, berauschend changierenden Nachrichten von der heftigen und frontalen Herausforderung unserer durch unsere eigene versunkene Wesenheit, der er dort begegnet.

Tilmann Haffke

start

: eine gefangene muse, zwei gefangene musen, drei gefangene ... museum !

gedanken zum anima-animal komplex in der kunst von dirk meinzer
(dm) für seine SIRENENHEIME ea in der kunsthalle göppingen,
vernissage am 17 mai 2009
zHd dr. annett reckert, marstallstrasse 55 in 73033 G.

hamburg, den 1. mai 2009

: nguva

ein tentatives logico-poeticum,
dargestellt wie plan und programm
oder traum
zu einem provisorischen mytherbarium
für visionspflanzen
(diter rot, da drinnen vor dem auge, suhrkamp 2005

ich habe mich euch im zustand der ungeschiedenen allverbundenheit gezeigt.
wo die seejungfer (halicore dugong, in china auch menschenfisch genannt)
sich tummelt, da ist der abgrund. wo das wasser ruht, da ist der abgrund.
wo das wasser kreist, da ist der abgrund. der abgrund hat neun namen.
diese waren drei davon.
(tschuang-tse, martin buber, manesse 1951

ich bin alles, weil ich (nur) fliessendes leben bin, und nichts als das.
ich bin unsterblich, weil aller tod in mich einmündet,
von dem des stockfisches (zum frühstück) bis zu dem von zeus.
in mir vereinigt werden sie wieder leben, das nicht mehr persönlich und
begrenzt ist, sondern panisch und daher frei.
(guiseppe tomasi di lampedusa, die sirene, piper 1961

ich stehe im täglichen dienst der kunst und mache das,
was getan werden muß: spielen !
(johnny „bad hair day" meese in art investor 03.09

aglaopheme: WILLKOMMEN in meiner kunst !

der erste eindruck beim betrachten der k von dm, der mich beschlich, war: hier ist einer,
der es gut mit mir meint: kein belehrender ton, keine anklage, kein cabaret, sondern
ernsthafte, consequente und stringente arbeit auf dem feld der k : dieser hermes zeigt mir,
was er ge- und empfunden hat im leben, macht es zum geschenk und fordert auf, mitzutun
(im schönsten deutschen sinne: hier bin ich mensch, hier darf ichs sein !

eine umarmung, keine berührungsängste, hingehen, ranziehen und aufessen, assimilieren
alchemistisches umwandeln: der elefantendung-krieger mikrokulturen spiegelphänomene
pointillistic watercolours, wald und wassergeister: die ahnengalerie der lächlers (self-)
portraits of (smiling) wood- and watersprites chimären-schimmel gruselkitschmännchen
wolpertinger die schiege (the geep)
dms pelztiercollection: furry fings diese skulpturen, mixed media collagen aus zb toten
maulwürfen, glasmurmeln, lametta, latexed potatoes with mummified flies and
nite-glo kids paint, grocery woods made from french fries, hot glue … schwimmen in der
unruhigen, schaumgeborenen dissonanten schönheit baudelaires: vereinige das
erschreckende reale mit dem grotesken idealen und mit glück erreichste den feuerhimmel
– als trüffelschwein des absonderlichen erzählt dm von der absurden schönheit des lebens
im spiegel des toten (rilkes sich im leben wähnen und doch umgeben sein von –

aus totem totems machen

dm als gastwirt gastgeber in seiner destille

die größe des raumes zwischen unsinn und tiefsee ausloten
: ein spiegel, der nicht zerbricht, gibt es das ? natürlich !
die spiegelfolie machts möglich. einfach auf wand, tür, hölzerne ikosaeder, kleiderschränke
aufkleben. lassen sie ihrer creativität frein lauf … dieser selbstklebende spiegel fängt
fliegen in jeder größe, läßt sich beliebig zuschneiden und bietet so unzählige anwendungs-
möglichkeiten. rückseitig mit raster bedruckt, damit sie die gewünschte form exact
zuschneiden können –

2

paradize umfriedete palmwedelhütte spiegelzelt, sternförmig
expressionistischer reichtum des spielerischen jonglierens
kleine, krummen gurken ähnnliche obszöne handschmeichler aus mundgeblasenem
tschechischem glas, in grün, schwarz, silbrig-glänzend, teils stachlig, teils sanft

gebogenes hurenkind *

dm ist im besten sinne ein un-intellektueller künstler: alles sackt zu boden, nichts bleibt
hängen im sieb des gedächtnisses, sondern die memen werden zu humus tief im inneren
des k, bis sie anfangen zu gären + geboren werden müssen 1 zeichner, die grenze ziehen
empfindsam überwältigt transgression exces rhizomorphe netze, handgeknüpft von
fischern in tansania, gehäkelt von der schwiegermutter, als immer blühender zimmergarten-
teppich geknotet in persien; das leuchtende auge des zyklopen bezeichnet das kunstwerk
verwinkelte zebra-zäune, selbst-genähte flugdrachen, cowboy-bootsies
totem-skulpturen: tote tiere nicht begraben, sondern aufstellen, um sich selbst zu sehen,
die lücke im blick des tieres als mittler des menschen zu seiner eigenen magischen
vergangenheit: hexer

muse – möse ?
den verzaubernden blick (baubo!) der vulva bannen durch das aufspiessen, micropussies:
schneemöschen im glas-sarg: thelxiope
und: dm gibt diesen obszönen mini-mösen durch seine „totalzensur" den zauber
des zarten zurück, des vermuteten statt des expliziten
(„ausgeschnittne pornoheftle")

re-start: himeropa

the sirenenheime-show by dirk meinzer @ kunsthalle goeppingen, germany

FROM LA GIOCONDA TO THE GEEP

: among the pickled (siren-) foetuses and bottled bones,
engaged in perfecting the catalogue, i found the last scion (…)

salutation
o generation of the thoroughly smug and thoroughly uncomfortable,
i have seen fishermen picnicking in the sun,
i have seen them with untidy families,
i have seen their smiles full of teeth and heard ungainly laughter.
and i am happier than you are, and they were happier than i am
and the fish swim in the lake and do not even own clothing.
(ezra pound, personae, 1926)

i see the fragmentary character of the world today with its prismatic nature of truth as
a chance, not a threat.
(alexander kluge in spex magazine, 09.07

small dead animals like mice and moles, marmels and silver tinsel, krokodilschwänze

je elaborierter die methoden, desto schwächer die subversion: the artworld tends to frame
new ideas in order to limit its possible effects, influence and eventual damage

spitzenklöppler vs. sturmwinddämonen: the intricacy of the lächlers, anfangs entstanden
vor ort in tansania aus im insomnia-furor erschlagenen fluginsekten, buchbinderleim,
lackedding, fluoreszierender kinder-glitzerfarbe und ganz vielen augen

punktebilder aus dem präapokalyptikum: wer zu lang in die sonne schaut, dem tanzen die
flirrenden lichtstrahlen auf der retina tango und das gesehene zerfällt in die einzelschritte
(van gogh ging in der mittaxhitze aufs feld und dm nachts in die discotheque, beschleunigt
unterm rasteraugenmond apollo suchen)

die berliner dugong.dvd: das schrundige ballett des somnambulen tieres, einladend,
mit hinabzutauchen in das aus dem mutterbauch erinnerte halluzinatorische trübe licht

kurz zur materialität: von titanweiß-ölfarbe auf mit leinwand bespanntem keilrahmen hin
zu getrockneten spaghetti auf plastikresten mit mäuseschädel ist in dms kunstkosmos alles
möglich, da es spricht: vom ephemeren, vom bleibenden, vom futilen, vom ... jetzt !
und jetzt !

charakteristisch für dms arbeit ist die haltung der umarmung: das hingehen, miterleben
und assimilieren (poiesis) – auch: das in-die-welt-geworfen-sein annehmen, sich nicht
zurück-verstecken wollen, sondern sich bewusst in der welt aussetzen; das fremde
begreift dm als ort der begegnung bzw. möglichkeit des wachsens – egal ob im rufiji-delta
in tansania, dem seythisfjördur-fjord auf island oder im kunstverein hamburg-st.pauli;
dieses zutiefst europäische moment des in der fremde seinen eigenen traditionen fremd
werden, damit man im staunen über die eigene unzulänglichkeit wieder mensch(lich) wird,
über sich selbst lacht ... findest du, liebe leserin, zb. im arsch-wackel-video, in dem dm
den in afrika gesehenen und mitgetanzten balztanz (girls only!) aufnimmt und lockt ...
teilzuhaben, loszulassen und sich einzulassen auf –

hier kommt also nun der humor ins spiel (lächlers

as a zeitgeist alchemist, dm is working in the intersection of myth and reality studying
famous and creating his own chimaerae, his nexus being the sireniae, both muse and
(very tasty !) seacow. their singing lured him repeatedly to africa (tanzania, sansibar),
where he lived, worked and very nearly found the halicore dugong (thats why
the dugong.dvd originates from the berliner tierpark in germany) – and, luckily for us,
he brought back home from africa the first lächler-paintings, small collages of slain
mosquitoes, hot glue, felt-tip pens and fluorescent nite-glo kids paint.

one main quality of dms work is EMBRACE: to go-see and assimilate the unknown
(poiesis) – meeting the strange, eating it up and producing beautiful art ... he recognizes
himself in the eyes of another (l'etranger, rimbaud, lacan) and, liking it, laughs about one's
own unfitness: everything ends in laughter.

das wiederholt auftauchende netz-motiv, dinglich und als übergeordnetes sinnstiftendes:
gezeichnet, gehäkelt, in den importierten fischernetzen aus tansania gegenüber … dms
vorstellung von kooperation, dem sich gegenseitig befruchten + in der verbindung
mehrerer köpfe etwas überraschendes zu schaffen (von den mikrokulturen-projekten bis
hin zu diesem text und unter deleuze' schirmherrschaft titelgebend den rhizomorphen
skulpturen, welche prompt wieder anfingen zu schimmeln und sich selbst zu machen;

the other stimulus of course is lamento

trotz? allen leidens an der gesellschaft, der neigung zur melancholischen verzweiflung
auf dem wc beim lesen von ciorans „vom nachteil, geboren zu sein" angesichts
der anforderungen, die das leben an einen stellt, trotz der versuchung, sich in der
transgression/exces batailles aufzulösen, (in dms worten: ach, ich bin auch eine sirene)
taucht in der bedrängnis, kurz vor dem verschwinden, wieder ein freundlicher blick,
1 befreiendes lachen in den k von dm auf: dm begreift das verschwinden nicht als
ausdruck des scheiterns, sondern als moment der höchsten lebendigkeit, aufgehoben
sein in der originalen vitalen dimension der existenz: ankommen im unbekannten,
endlich undoder: das irreale chaos erlöst von der beengenden realität (nochmal baudelaire)

lächlers – FROM MONA LISA TO ACID (gesichter haben): diese naiv-grazilen,
fein geschichteten portraits von bekannten und geträumten, metaphysische mischwesen in
der tradition max ernst' und paul klees tanzen auf der grenze von schönheit und alter,
potenz und flatulenz – sie lachen der vergänglichkeit ins gesicht !

delicately modeled graces from the underworld,
they are a classic po-mo vanitas ensemble

rhizomorphic landscapes or food forests: decomposing and restructuring as a
work principle – these sculptures, made from french fries, latexed potatoes, cucumber
and tomatoes, dried spaghetti, acrylic color, anglerspezialbedarf, christmasglitter,
having been layered with for years, growing and changing, decay, evaporate with a big
stink, remodeling themselves while maturing and inviting on their way to shipwreck flies,
funghi and other lifeforms to root + make themselves at home in these k –
they finish themselves (off).

3

molpe

schnelles zebra, der geisterfischer :

der unmögliche versuch, angemessen von 2 (4?) kunstwerken dms zu schreiben, als da
wären ein 3teiliger gehäkelter wollpyjama mit mütze, schwarzweiss gestreift und 2 neue
acquarelle aus der lächler-serie, alle entstanden in kooperation mit familie anke wenzel :

der 3teilige wollanzug, ein grotesk heimeliges, hochästhetisches objekt, selbstgehäkelt,
schwarzweiss gestreift; das langärmelige grobmaschige oberteil, mit v-ausschnitt und
angenähtem schultergurt für den pfeileköcher? sowie bedrohlicher kriegermaske auf
bauchhöhe mit 2 stechenden punktaugen (ich bin besessen / in mir gärt es wieder
UND ES WILL RAUS !) erscheint eher kuschelweich zum sich anschmiegen einzuladen
als aggressiv-schützend das jagen zu ermöglichen; ebenso wirkt der mützenkopf mit
seinem fransigen bart und dem pinken pickel am kinn deutlich weniger januskräftig,
den bösen blick mittels zweiten gesichts nach rückwärts hin bändigen zu können,
als ihm übers haar streichen oder ihn eigentlich umarmen zu müssen;

die beiden gerahmten zeichnungen hängen nebeneinander auf augenhöhe an der wand und
blicken dem betrachter direkt ins gesicht, sie besitzen jeweils nur ein auge, eine dicke nase
und einen zum sprechen – munchisch schreiend ? geöffneten mund mit dicken lippen
– hinter und vor der weißnebligen geistererscheinung liegen vielfarbige rautenflächen,
in auflösung begriffen, auseinanderdriftend ? eben explodiert ? unklar ist, ob die
gespenstig-totenköpfigen gerade erscheinen (krafft-ebing, schreck-nötzing ?) oder dabei
sind, zu verschwinden, der abdruck eines schattens auf mathematischem spezialpapier ?

der linke, nicht so stark vom mottenfraß? befallene kopf wird zusätzlich gehalten von
einer fein-maschigen gitternetzstruktur (craquelé ? – ein gefangener, nach luft
schnappender fisch

zusammen ein nicht eben beruhigendes paar, das seine sprengkraft aber sehr geschickt hinter der harmlos-vertrauten materialität der heimarbeit versteckt und von seinen ängsten erzählend auf erlösung im mitfühlenden auge des betrachters hofft –

–

nguva is kisuaheli for siren
aglaopheme : die süße-rede sirene (griech.)
thelxiope : die bezaubernd aussehende sirene (auch griech.)
himeropa : the soft-voice siren (greek)
molpe : die singende sirene

ende

c t.man 2009 allesgraumiau(at)hotmail.de by licence to dirk meinzer

psst: noch 2 boni !
: unterhaltung mit der sirene: nur kopf (mit silbernem kamm)
und hals (war aufgetaucht). „du bist hübsch." entschied sie. „du auch !"
beeilte ich mich, und sie rümpfte befriedigt die nase: „na.", und „fühl ma'!". ihre haut war
allerdings wie ganz zartes seidenpapier, aber nicht faltig unangenehm, und ich sagte das
sofort: „wenn du überall so wärst …".
„ja: wenn!! …" knurrte sie tief (seelöwig) und erbittert
(beruhigte sich aber bald wieder). arno schmidt 16.8.1955
und
: ich suchte ein dach, meine federn zu trocknen.
bekanntlich tragen sirenen federn.
und der sommerhimmel 2009 war nass und kalt und für federvieh
eine zumutung. für weisses federvieh besonders.
– war eine gerupfte sirene ein mensch ?
(irmtraut morgner,
der schöne und das biest

ANHANG
APPENDIX

Biographie / Biography

1972 geboren in Karlsruhe / born 1972 in Karlsruhe

Ausbildung / education

1997–2004 Studium und Diplom der Freien Kunst bei Claus Böhmler, Hochschule für bildende Künste Hamburg

1996 / 97 Studium der Philosophie an der Humboldt-Universität zu Berlin

1995 / 96 Studium der Betriebswirtschaft an der Hochschule für Technik und Wirtschaft Berlin

Stipendien / scholarships

2009 Atelier- und Arbeitsstipendium der Sparkassen-Kulturstiftung Stormarn

2008 / 2009 Atelierstipendium Goldbekhaus, Hamburg

2006 Hamburger Arbeitsstipendium für Bildende Kunst, Hamburg

2003 / 2004 Reisestipendium der Studienstiftung des Deutschen Volkes für Tansania

2004 / 2005 Begabtenförderstipendium der Hochschule für bildende Künste Hamburg

2001–2003 Stipendium der Studienstiftung des Deutschen Volkes

Veröffentlichungen / Publications

Vermessung, exh. cat., Schloss Agathenburg, Kunsthalle Faust, edition: 700, 2009

Index, exh. cat., Kunsthaus Hamburg, 2007, p. 18

Terrain vague: wheely, exh. cat., Bonner Kunstverein, Wiehl 2007

So nah. So fern. So fern. So nah, exh. cat., Schloss Agathenburg, Palais für aktuelle Kunst Glückstadt, Hamburg 2007, p. 16ff

Ich sehe Land, exh. cat., Mayerhof, Wien 2006

Das Pferd in der zeitgenössischen Kunst, exh. cat., Kunsthalle Göppingen, Ostfildern 2006, p. 76f

Dirk Meinzer, *Sirenenheime III. Bin schon weg. Künstlerische Feldforschung in Tansania,* in *Kultur und Gespenster, Nr. 1,* 2006, pp. 222–253

Don't accept mañana, exh. cat., Kunstverein Braunschweig, Abteimünsterschwarzach 2006, pp. 56f

Kunstlicht Kongress, exh. cat., Berlin, 2004

spur 04. the cheap champagne issue x, Hochschule für Bildende Künste Hamburg, 2004, pp. 110–113

Ausstellungsraum Taubenstrasse 13, exh. cat., Berlin 2002, pp. 76f, 162, 166f

»re // MIR« Artist – Communication, exh. cat., Hamburg–St. Petersburg 2001, Hamburg

Rundgang 4–7 Change is good; my world is not enough; Flexibilitätsversuche; German Leitkultur, exh. cat., Spangenberg, 2001, p. 51

Künstlerbücher / artist books

Lächler, entstanden im Rahmen des Arbeitsstipendiums der Stadt Hamburg / created during the scholarship of Hamburg, edition: 120, Hamburg 2006

Transgression / excess, im Selbstverlag / self-published, edition: 400, Hamburg 2003

Mikrokulturen, im Selbstverlag / self-published, edition: 400, 1999

Ausstellungen / Exhibitions

Einzelausstellungen / solo exhibitions

2009

Sirenenheime, Kunsthalle Göppingen
argante abrasdel, Bomba Bomba, with Anke Wenzel,
Kunstverein St. Pauli, Hamburg

2008

Wer lange in die Sonne schaut,
Ferenbalm-Gurbrü Station, Karlsruhe

2007

Lächler, Galerie Olaf Stüber, Berlin

2006

Sirenenheime, Jonathan Meese-Foyer,
Volksbühne Berlin
Sirenenheime II, with Anke Wenzel, Agentur für
zeitgenössische Kunst, Hamburg

2004

Bin schon weg, with Nicola Torke,
Galerie Nomadenoase, Hamburg

2002

instantart, with Tjorg Beer, artgenda, Hamburg

2001

easy-easy foundation / Brüten, Galerie 88, Hamburg

2000

Wer zu lange in die Sonne schaut...,
Ausstellungsraum Taubenstrasse, Hamburg

Gruppenausstellungen / group exhibitions

2009

Fantastisch, Städtische Galerie Pforzheim
Swinging on the Wrecking Ball,
Kooperation der Galerien Ferenbalm-Gurbrü Station und
Galerie Margit Haupt, Karlsruhe
Vermessung, Schloss Agathenburg,
Kunsthalle Faust, Hannover
Borderline Pleasure, Galerie Michael Janssen, Berlin
Los soñadores, Velada Santa Lucía, Maracaibo, Venezuela

2008

Max Ernst. Surrealismus / A l'intérieur de la vue,
Kunsthalle Göppingen
Wir nennen es Hamburg, Kunstverein Hamburg
Moral Tarantula 2, Elektrohaus, Hamburg
Walk through, Hamburg
Tiere – Tierbilder, Schloss Filseck, Göppingen
space other at other spaces 01: Hipódromo 610,
Galería Candela, San Juan, Puerto Rico
Expanded Painting, Space Other, Boston, USA
LA is on fire, David Lawrence Gallery, Los Angeles, USA

2007

Ornament und Verbrechen,
Galerie Nikolaus Bischoff, Lahr
A und O, Galerie Jürgen Becker, Hamburg
Fish & Chips, Kunsthaus Hamburg
So fern. So nah. Begegnungen mit der Fremde,
Palais für aktuelle Kunst, Glückstadt
Ginnungagap / Pavilion of Belief,
Galerie im Regierungsviertel, Venedig, Italien
Grüsse aus dem Durcheinandertal,
Galerie Brachmanns Galeron, Hamburg
Who, Kunstverein Hamburg
Artists' Books: Transgression / Excess,
Space Other, Boston, USA

2006

Common Sense, Ausstellungsraum 25, Zürich, Schweiz
Afrique, il y a foi, Galerie Olaf Stüber, Berlin
Terrain Vague: wheely, Kunstverein Bonn
Ich sehe Land, Festival Waldhausen, Österreich
Vom Pferd erzählen, Kunsthalle Göppingen

2005

Mami Wata's easy-easy foundation, Kunst und Kultur in der Hafencity, Hamburg
Don't accept mañana, Kunstverein Braunschweig
re-escape, temporäre Kunstprojekte im öffentlichen Raum, Hamburg
microscopium, message salon, Zürich, Schweiz
Reykjavik Art Festival, Dieter Roth Akademie, Reykjavik Art Museum, Island

2004

Kunstlichtkongress, Kunstraum Walcheturm, Zürich, Schweiz
Dieter Roth Academy and friends, St. Petri, Lübeck

2003

Saturnopticum, Taubenstrasse, Kunstverein Harburg
transgression / excès theatre production with Malte Ubenauf, Kampnagel Hamburg

2002

Dieter Roth Akademie, Atelier Dieter Roth, Reykjavik
Endlichter, Künstlerhaus Weidenallee, Hamburg

2001

German Leitkultur, Kunsthalle Fridericianum, Kassel
re-mir, borey-art gallery, St. Petersburg, Russland
re-mir II, art agents gallery, Hamburg
Schwindel, Ausstellungsraum Taubenstrasse, Hamburg
Mikrokulturen II, Künstlerhaus Weidenallee, Hamburg

1999

Mikrokulturen I, awarded the Ditze-price, Hochschule für bildende Künste Hamburg

Verzeichnis der abgebildeten Werke / List of works depicted

Seit Mai 2009, in Zusammenhang mit dieser Publikation, erfasst Lara Eva Sochor (L.S.) das Werk von Dirk Meinzer.

Beginning in May 2009, Lara Eva Sochor (L.S.) compiled the catalogue of Dirk Meinzer's works for this publication.

1. *Saturnoptikum*, 2003–2009
Transparentspiegelfolie, Holz, Metall
Two-way mirror film, wood, metal
380 × 120 × 240 cm
L.S. 2009/57

2. *Kumbi-Kumbi Sturmwinddämon*, 2004
Insektenflügel, Leim, Lack auf Pappe
Insect wings, glue, lacquer on paper
24 × 18 cm
Private collection
L.S. 2009/137

3. *Sturmwinddämon Himmel*, 2005
Insektenflügel, Leim, Lack auf Pappe
Insect wings, glue, lacquer on paper
23 × 17 cm
Andrea Tippel
L.S. 2009/134

4. *Sturmwinddämon I*, 2004
Insektenflügel, Leim
Insect wings, glue
19,5 × 15 cm
Ben Hübsch
L.S. 2009/123

5. *upepo V*, 2006
Insektenflügel, Leim
Insect wings, glue
15 × 10 cm
Private collection
L.S. 2009/27

6. *Sturmwinddämon III*, 2004
Insektenflügel, Leim
Insect wings, glue
15,5 × 20 cm
Courtesy Galerie Nikolaus Bischoff
L.S. 2009/125

7. *Sturmwinddämon II*, 2004
Insektenflügel, Leim
Insect wings, glue
12,5 × 10 cm
Courtesy Galerie Nikolaus Bischoff
L.S. 2009/124

8. *kleiner Sturmwinddämon*, 2004
Insektenflügel, Leim, Lack auf Pappe
Insect wings, glue, lacquer on paper
11 × 9 cm
L.S. 2009/135

9. *dunkler Sturmwinddämon*, 2004
Insektenflügel, Leim, Lack auf Pappe
Insect wings, glue, lacquer on paper
18 × 15 cm
L.S. 2009/136

10. *upepo I*, 2005
Fluoreszentes, Mücken auf Papier
Fluorescent paint, midges on paper
14 × 11 cm
Private collection
L.S. 2009/28

11. *upepo II*, 2005
Fluoreszentes, Mücken auf Papier
Fluorescent paint, midges on paper
14,5 × 10 cm
Private collection
L.S. 2009/29

12. *upepo IV*, 2006
Fluoreszentes, Mücken auf Papier
Fluorescent paint, midges on paper
14 × 12 cm
Private collection
L.S. 2009/26

13. *Fliegengezwitscher I*, 2006
Stubenfliegen, verschiedene Materialien
Houseflies, mixed media
14 × 12 cm
Private collection
L.S. 2009/23

14. *Fliegengezwitscher II*, 2006
Stubenfliegen, verschiedene Materialien
Houseflies, mixed media
14 × 12 cm
Private collection
L.S. 2009/24

15. *Sternmullgeist*, 2006
Maulwurfschädel, verschiedene Materialien
Mole skull, mixed media
17 × 11 cm
Private collection
L.S. 2009/25

16. *ithyphallic cucumber*, 1999
mit Hausratte / with house rat
Gurke, Buchbinderleim
Cucumber, bookbinding glue
52 × 40 × 36 cm
L.S. 2009/100

17. *Kartoffeltiger*, 2006
mit Ratte / with rat
Buchbinderleim, Kartoffeln, Strass, Toast
Bookbinding glue, potatoes, diamante, toast
14 × 12 × 9 cm
Courtesy Galerie Olaf Stüber
L.S. 2009/153

18. *einäugiger Januskopf*, 2008
Buchbinderleim, Salat, Adlerfedern
Bookbinding glue, lettuce, eagle feathers
42 × 20 × 19 cm
Sammlung Kunsthalle Göppingen
L.S. 2009/51

19. *Kartoffelkrieger*, 2007
Buchbinderleim, Kartoffeln, verschiedene Materialien
Bookbinding glue, potatoes, mixed media
21 × 27 × 7 cm
L.S. 2009/97

20. *Dungkrieger*, 2007
Elefantendung, Zement, Alu, Geierflaum
Elephant dung, cement, aluminium, vulture down
89 × 41 × 23 cm
Courtesy Galerie Olaf Stüber
L.S. 2009/47

21. *blauer Tod*, 2009
Styropor, Fluoreszentes, Pfauenfedern, Glasaugen, verschiedene Materialien
Polystyrene, fluorescent paint, peacock feathers, glass eyes, mixed media
39 × 33 × 17 cm
Courtesy Ferenbalm-Gurbrü Station
L.S. 2009/101

22. *dreibeinige Eule*, 2007
Kaimanschwanz, Glasaugen, Lack, Plastik auf Plexi
Caiman tail, glass eyes, lacquer, plastic on perspex
32 × 16 × 15 cm
Ignacio López, San Juan, Puerto Rico
L.S. 2009/52

23. *Katze*, 1999
Wolle, Wachs
Wool, wax
9 × 14 × 15 cm
Private collection
L.S. 2009/10

24. *Mäuslesarg*, 2007
Plastik, Gips, Acryl, Lack, Fluoreszentes, Ponpons
Plastic Plaster, acrylic, lacquer, fluorescent paint, pompoms
14 × 13 × 7 cm
Private collection
L.S. 2009/11

25. *Hasenmond*, 2005
Acryl, Aluminium, Pommes, Hasenfell
Acrylic, aluminium, chips, hare fur
20 × 15 × 3 cm
Courtesy Ferenbalm-Gurbrü Station
L.S. 2009/114

26. *Fritz's Baumgeist*, 2006
Polyester, Pommes, Ponpons, Glasaugen, verschiedene Materialien
Polyester, chips, pompoms, glass eyes, mixed media
28 × 18 × 14 cm
Courtesy Galerie Nikolaus Bischoff
L.S. 2009/99

27. *Ohne Titel,* 2007
Pommes, Buchbinderleim, Heißkleber, Lack, verschiedene Materialien
Chips, bookbinding glue, hot glue, lacquer, mixed media
37 × 14 × 14 cm
Private collection
L.S. 2009/9

28. *Pommeskapelle,* 2007
Pommes, Heißkleber, Seifenfiguren, verschiedene Materialien auf Plexi
Chips, hot glue, soap forms, various materials on perspex
25 × 21 × 33 cm
Courtesy Galerie Olaf Stüber
L.S. 2009/56

29. *Heller Baumgeist,* 2007
Menschenhaar, Acryl, Glasaugen
Human hair, acrylic, glass eyes
53 × 20 × 20 cm
Courtesy Galerie Olaf Stüber
L.S. 2009/39

30. *Präapokalyptikum / 2. Ordnung,* 2007
Körperbehaarung, verschiedene Materialien
Body hair, mixed media
38 × 11 × 8 cm
Courtesy Galerie Olaf Stüber
L.S. 2009/168

31. *Beflügelte Spitze,* 2008
Wachs, Plastik, Seife
Wax, plastic, soap
21 × 18 × 15 cm
L.S. 2009/170

32. *Bunny M,* 2008
Seife, Ponpons, Holz, Kronentaubenfeder
Soap, pompoms, wood, crowned-pigeon feather
20 × 7 × 7 cm
L.S. 2009/156

33. *romantische Spaghetti I,* 2008
Spaghetti, Buchbinderleim, Draht, Fluoreszentes
Spaghetti, bookbinding glue, wire, fluorescent paint
40 × 20 × 20 cm
Private collection
L.S. 2009/53

34. *romantische Spaghetti II,* 2008
Spaghetti, Buchbinderleim, Schaumstoff, Fluoreszentes
Spaghetti, bookbinding glue, foam, fluorescent paint
10 × 25 × 15 cm
Courtesy Galerie Olaf Stüber
L.S. 2009/54

35. *Elster, denkend,* 2009
Elsterkopf, Trauben, Leim, verschiedene Materialien
Magpie head, grapes, glue, mixed media
20 × 14 × 8 cm
Courtesy Ferenbalm-Gurbrü Station
L.S. 2009/157

36. *Lilit,* 2009
Tierpräparate verleimt, verschiedene Materialien
Glued animal specimens, mixed media
27 × 10,5 × 10,5 cm
Courtesy Ferenbalm-Gurbrü Station
L.S. 2009/96

37. *animierter Grund,* 2009
Buchbinderleim, Äpfel, Karotten, Glasaugen, verschiedene Materialien
Bookbinding glue, apples, carrots, glass eyes, mixed media
39 × 33 × 17 cm
L.S. 2009/98

38. *grüner Lächler,* 2007
Ölpastellkreide auf Papier
Oil pastel on paper
29,5 × 19 cm
Courtesy Galerie Jürgen Becker
L.S. 2009/139

39. *Lächler Vierauge II,* 2008
Ölwachskreide auf Papier
Oil pastel on paper
24 × 21 cm
Private collection
L.S. 2009/17

40. *Lächler Vierauge I,* 2008
Ölwachskreide auf Papier
Oil pastel on paper
26 × 25 cm
Private collection
L.S. 2009/16

41. *Lächler (Du!),* 2007
Ölpastellkreide auf Papier
Oil pastel on paper
30 × 21 cm
Felix Krebs
L.S. 2009/129

42. *Lächler (Du!),* 2007
Ölpastellkreide auf Papier
Oil pastel on paper
30 × 27 cm
Felix Krebs
L.S. 2009/130

43. *Pink Mond,* 2004
Acryl, Lack auf Leinwand
Acrylic, lacquer on canvas
100 × 80 cm
Private collection
L.S. 2009/174

44. *Lächler argante II,* 2007
Ölwachspastell auf Papier
Oil pastel on paper
28 × 22 cm
Gabriel Torke
L.S. 2009/148

45. *Höllenpopanz,* 2006
Acryl, Lack, Öl, Fluoreszentes auf Holz
Acrylic, lacquer, oil, fluorescent paint on wood
32 × 27 cm
Private collection
L.S. 2009/138

46. *Lächler Vierauge,* 2006
Ölpastellkreide auf Papier
Oil pastel on paper
40 × 25 cm
Private collection
L.S. 2009/126

47. *dunkla Geist,* 2007
Öl auf Leinwand
Oil on canvas
90 × 90 cm
Private collection
L.S. 2009/162

48. *Lächler,* 2006
Ölpastellkreide auf Papier
Oil pastel on paper
28 × 21 cm
Gora Jain
L.S. 2009/132

49. *Modder-Lächler,* 2008
Ölwachskreide auf Papier
Oil pastel on paper
28 × 20 cm
Private collection
L.S. 2009/8

50. *Elephrontal,* 2006
Acryl, Öl auf Pappe
Acrylic, oil on card
79 × 59 cm
Andrea Tippel
L.S. 2009/133

51. *Colonel Fabien,* 2007
Aquarell, Lack, Tusche
Watercolour, lacquer, Indian ink
30 × 21 cm
L.S. 2009/120

52. *Wolkenpopanz,* 2007
Ölwachskreide auf Papier
Oil pastel on paper
26 × 17 cm
Private collection, USA
L.S. 2009/149

53. *Sonnenpopanz,* 2007
Ölwachskreide auf Papier
Oil pastel on paper
39 × 29 cm
Private collection, USA
L.S. 2009/150

54. *Punktegeist II,* 2006
Ölwachskreide auf Papier in Plexiglas
Oil pastel on paper in perspex
40 × 28 cm
Courtesy Galerie Jürgen Becker
L.S. 2009/147

55. *lächelndes Auge,* 2006
Ölpastellkreide auf Papier
Oil pastel on paper
32,5 × 27 cm
Courtesy Ferenbalm-Gurbrü Station
L.S. 2009/112

56. *Punktegeist,* 2007
Ölwachskreide auf Papier
Oil pastel on paper
33 × 23 cm
Private collection
L.S. 2009/21

57. *Punktegeist,* 2007
Pastellkreide auf Karton
Pastel on cardboard
56 × 42 cm
Courtesy Galerie Olaf Stüber
L.S. 2009/116

58. *Hexe Lächlerin,* 2007
Ölwachspastell auf Papier
Oil pastel on paper
31 × 24 cm
L.S. 2009/177

59. *Froschgeist,* 2008
Ölwachskreide auf Papier
Oil pastel on paper
30 × 23 cm
Private collection
L.S. 2009/20

60. *Schweinegeist,* 2007
Ölwachskreide auf Papier
Oil pastel on paper
30 × 23 cm
Private collection
L.S. 2009/22

61. *Versaillegeist,* 2007
Ölwachskreide auf Papier
Oil pastel on paper
31 × 22 cm
Courtesy Ferenbalm-Gurbrü Station
L.S. 2009/151

62. *Lichtknecht II,* 2008
Ölpastellkreide auf Papier
Oil pastel on paper
30,5 × 20,5 cm
Oda und Roland Bischoff
L.S. 2009/119

63. *Lichtknecht I,* 2008
Ölpastellkreide auf Papier
Oil pastel on paper
29 × 21 cm
Private collection
L.S. 2009/118

64. *witchbitch,* 2008
Öl, Pastellkreide, Tusche auf Leinwand
Oil, pastel, Indian ink on canvas
54 × 44 cm
Courtesy Ferenbalm-Gurbrü Station
L.S. 2009/115

65. *witchbitch II,* 2009
mit / with Axel Heil, fluid editions Basel
handpigmentierter Chromalindruck, Zeichnung
Hand-coloured chromalin print, drawing
Auflage / edition: 20
20 × 20 cm
L.S. 2009/178, 179, 180, 181, 182, 202
Private collection

66. *Graupopanz I,* 2009
mit / with Anke Wenzel
Aquarell, Tusche auf Papier
Watercolour, Indian ink on paper
29 × 21 cm
Courtesy Galerie Nikolaus Bischoff
L.S. 2009/154

67. *Graupopanz II,* 2009
mit / with Anke Wenzel
Aquarell, Tusche auf Papier
Watercolour, Indian ink on paper
29 × 21 cm
Courtesy Ferenbalm-Gurbrü Station
L.S. 2009/155

68. *Höllengeistmeinzimani I,* 2008
Acryl, Fluoreszentes, Lack, verschiedene Materialien
Acrylic, fluorescent paint, lacquer, mixed media
28 × 21 cm
Private collection
L.S. 2009/18

69. *gelber Leberlächler*, 2008
Ölwachskreide auf Papier
Oil pastel on paper
29 × 21 cm
Courtesy Ferenbalm-Gurbrü Station
L.S. 2009/113

70. *Wassergeist*, 2005
verschiedene Materialien auf Folie
Various materials on transparency film
26 × 18 cm
Courtesy Galerie Nikolaus Bischoff
L.S. 2009/122

71. *Punktegeist I / 2.Ordnung*, 2009
Papier, Monotypie, Lack
Paper, monotype, lacquer
40 × 29 cm
Courtesy Galerie Olaf Stüber
L.S. 2009/163

72. *Punktegeist II / 2.Ordnung*, 2009
Papier, Monotypie, Lack
Paper, monotype, lacquer
40 × 29 cm
L.S. 2009/164

73. *Kupferkopf*, 2009
Ölwachskreide auf Papier
Oil pastel on paper
30 × 21 cm
Private collection
L.S. 2009/15

74. *Präapokalyptikum I*, 2001
Neonklebepunkte auf Pappe
Adhesive neon dots on card
76 × 110 cm
Private collection
L.S. 2009/70

75. *Präapokalyptikum III*, 2004
Neonklebepunkte auf Pappe
Adhesive neon dots on card
47 × 66 cm
Private collection
L.S. 2009/72

76. *Präapokalyptikum IV*, 2004
Neonklebepunkte auf Pappe
Adhesive neon dots on card
47 × 66 cm
Private collection
L.S. 2009/73

77. *Präapokalyptikum V*, 2005
Neonklebepunkte auf Pappe
Adhesive neon dots on card
47 × 66 cm
Private collection
L.S. 2009/74

78. *Präapokalyptikum VIII*, 2007
Neonklebepunkte auf Pappe
Adhesive neon dots on card
47 × 66 cm
Private collection
L.S. 2009/76

79. *Präapokalyptikum X*, 2007
Neonklebepunkte auf Pappe
Adhesive neon dots on card
48 × 68 cm
Private collection
L.S. 2009/77

80. *rascha-rascha Somanga II*, 2005
Aquarell auf Pappe
Watercolour on card
30 × 35 cm
Private collection
L.S. 2009/14

81. *Utete*, 2004
Filzstift und Lack auf Papier
Felt pen and lacquer on paper
14 × 21 cm
L.S. 2009/176

82. *rascha-rascha Somanga I*, 2005
Aquarell auf Pappe
Watercolour on card
30 × 40 cm
Private collection
L.S. 2009/13

83. *Nguva*, 2004
Lack, Aquarell auf Papier
Lacquer, watercolour on paper
15 × 14 cm
L.S. 2009/175

84. *upepo ya kassa*, 2004
Schildpatt, Lack
Tortoise shell, lacquer
7 × 9 cm
L.S. 2009/171

85. *Somanga*, 2005
Filzstift auf Papier
Felt pen on paper
21 × 15 cm
Courtesy Galerie Nikolaus Bischoff
L.S. 2009/30

86. *rascha-rascha I*, 2004
KILWA MASOKO SIRENENHEIME
Filzstift, Aquarell, Lack, Tusche, Papier auf Pappe aufgezogen
Felt pen, watercolour, lacquer, Indian ink, paper on cardboard
19 × 14 cm
Andrea Tippel
L.S. 2009/33

87. *rascha-rascha (kleiner Regen) II*, 2005
Filzstift, Lack, Aquarell,
Papier auf Pappe aufgezogen
Felt pen, lacquer, watercolour,
paper on cardboard
21 × 14 cm
Private collection
L.S. 2009/128

88. *Matema*, 2005
mit / with Anke Wenzel
Acryl auf Leinwand
Acrylic on canvas
120 × 80 cm
L.S. 2009/108

89. *rascha-rascha argante*, 2006
Lack auf Folie
Lacquer on transparency film
26 × 18 cm
Astrid und Christoph Grau
L.S. 2009/131

90. *Rufiji-Geist*, 2005
Aquarell auf Papier
Watercolour on paper
21 × 15 cm
Courtesy Galerie Nikolaus Bischoff
L.S. 2009/34

91. *rascha-rascha III*, 2005
Filzstift, Aquarell auf Papier
Felt pen, watercolour on paper
10,5 × 8,5 cm
Courtesy Galerie Nikolaus Bischoff
L.S. 2009/31

92. *Bwejuu*, 2005
Tusche auf Papier
Indian ink on paper
21 × 15 cm
Private collection
L.S. 2009/172

93. *waoKönig*, 2006
Segeltuch, Glasfaserstäbe, Lack, Fluoreszentes
Sailcloth, glass-fibre rods, lacquer, fluorescent paint
210 × 200 cm
Private collection, USA
L.S. 2009/65

94. *little cloud I*, 2007
mit / with Anke Wenzel
Segeltuch, Kohlefaserstäbe, Glasaugen
Sailcloth, carbon-fibre rods, glass eyes
180 × 160 cm
L.S. 2009/66

95. *little cloud II*, 2008
mit / with Anke Wenzel
Segeltuch, Kohlefaserstäbe, Windeln
Sailcloth, carbon-fibre rods, nappies
180 × 160 cm
L.S. 2009/67

96. *little dark cloud / Motte*, 2008
mit / with Anke Wenzel
Segeltuch, Kohlefaserstäbe
Sailcloth, carbon-fibre rods
180 × 160 × 30 cm
L.S. 2009/68

97. *Poplife / vom Nachteil geboren zu sein*, 2007
Holz, Gips, Draht, Lack, Wolle, Fluoreszentes, Stubenfliegen, Glasauge, Spiegel, Bambus, Kokospalmwedel
Wood, plaster of Paris, wire, lacquer, wool, fluorescent paint, houseflies, glass eyes, mirror, bamboo, coconut palm fronds
210 × 60 × 24 cm
Private collection
L.S. 2009/37

98. *Grüner Geist*, 2007
Hausmäuse, Kamelhaar, Ponpons, Fluoreszentes
House mice, camel hair, pompoms, fluorescent paint
30,5 × 26 × 6,5 cm
Courtesy Ferenbalm-Gurbrü Station
L.S. 2009/35

99. *Steingeist*, 2007
Wismut, Plexi, Lack, verschiedene Materialien auf Aludibond
Bismuth, perspex, lacquer, mixed media on Aludibond
35 × 21 × 20 cm
L.S. 2009/38

100. *Theiresiasgeist*, 2007
Glasaugen, Museumskäfer, Buchbinderleim, Plexi, verschiedene Materialien
Glass eyes, museum beetle, bookbinding glue, perspex, mixed media
32 × 22 × 9 cm
Courtesy Galerie Olaf Stüber
L.S. 2009/36

101. *Wilder Geist I*, 2008
Mausschädel, Glasaugen, Stubenfliegen auf Plexi
Mouse skull, glass eyes, houseflies on perspex
25,5 × 17,5 cm
Sammlung Kunsthalle Göppingen
L.S. 2009/41

102. *Wilder Geist II*, 2008
Plastik, Motte, Glasaugen, Stubenfliegen auf Plexi
Plastic, moths, glass eyes, houseflies on perspex
24 × 17 cm
Sammlung Kunsthalle Göppingen
L.S. 2009/42

103. *Wassergeist V*, 2008
Acryl, Plastik, Lack, Fluoreszentes, Glasaugen, Schwärmer
Acrylic, plastic, lacquer, fluorescent paint, glass eyes, hawk moths
30 × 30 × 9 cm
L.S. 2009/40

104. *Nesthäckchen*, 2008
Elster, Diamantfasan, Kaiman, Glasauge, Plastik
Magpie, Lady Amherst's Pheasant, caiman, glass eye, plastic
26 × 25 cm
Courtesy Galerie Nikolaus Bischoff
L.S. 2009/43

105. *Vögeligeist*, 2008
Eisvogel, Glasauge, Spaghetti, Buchbinderleim, Plastikfolie auf Plexi
Kingfisher, glass eye, spaghetti, bookbinding glue, transparency film on perspex
32 × 28 cm
Susanne und Dirk Dobke
L.S. 2009/44

106. *Mimi*, 2008
Diverse Tierpräparate auf Plexi, verschiedene Materialien
Various animal specimens on perspex, mixed media
31 × 21 cm
Courtesy Galerie Olaf Stüber
L.S. 2009/103

107. *Mäuslegeist*, 2006
Neonklebepunkte, Leim, Maus, Mottenflügel, Glasauge, Ponpons, Fluoreszentes, Glitterfäden
Adhesive neon dots, glue, mouse, moth wings, glass eye, pompoms, fluorescent paint, glitter threads
24 × 11 cm
Clarissa Labin
L.S. 2009/46

108. *little dark mousecloud*, 2008
Stubenfliegenkuchen, Hausmaus, Buchbinderleim, Ponpons, Plexi, verschiedene Materialien
Housefly cake, house mouse, bookbinding glue, pompoms, perspex, mixed media
30 × 24 × 7 cm
Courtesy Galerie Olaf Stüber
L.S. 2009/48

109. *Windschättin,* 2008
Fasanbalg, Fledermaus, Nachtfalter
Pheasant skin, bat, moth
34 × 34 cm
Courtesy Galerie Nikolaus Bischoff
L.S. 2009/45

110. *Windschättin II,* 2009
Pfeilschwanzkrebs, Schwärmer, Fuchsschwanz,
verschiedene Materialien
Horseshoe crab, hawk moth, fox tail, mixed media
41 × 29 cm
Courtesy Ferenbalm-Gurbrü Station
L.S. 2009/102

111. *Sylphe,* 2008
Stubenfliegenkuchen, Speckkäferlarven, Fluoreszentes,
Adlerdaunen, Leim auf Plexi
Housefly cake, carpet beetle larvae, fluorescent paint,
eagle down, glue on perspex
40 × 22 × 6 cm
Courtesy Galerie Olaf Stüber
L.S. 2009/49

112. *Gigi Glücksgeist,* 2009
Ölwachskreide auf Pappe, Kakerlaken,
Babypfeilschwanzkrebs
Oil pastel on card, cockroaches, baby horseshoe crab
69 × 49 cm
Courtesy Ferenbalm-Gurbrü Station
L.S. 2009/173

113. *Sonnenshowa,* 2009
Acryl, Öl, Fluoreszentes, Schmetterlinge auf Leinwand
Acrylic, oil, fluorescent paint, butterflies on canvas
120 × 80 cm
Henriette von Saldern
L.S. 2009/127

114. *Punktegeist IV,* 2008
Neonklebepunkte, verschiedene Materialien auf Plexi
Adhesive neon dots, mixed media on perspex
27 × 25 cm
Private collection
L.S. 2009/142

115. *Schau mir in die Augen, Kleines,* 2009
mit / with Tilmann Haffke
Pappe, Bauschaum, verschiedene Materialien
Card, building foam, mixed media
30 × 24 cm
Courtesy Galerie Olaf Stüber
L.S. 2009/143

116. *Babiganushi,* 2008
Kaimanschwanz, Glasaugen, Lack, Plastik auf Plexi
Caiman tail, glass eyes, lacquer, plastic on perspex
25 × 20 × 17 cm
Private collection
L.S. 2009/50

117. *Mexikanisches Gelächter,* 2009
Stiefel, Holz, Styropor
Boots, wood, polystyrene
134 × 35 × 23 cm
Courtesy Ferenbalm-Gurbrü Station
L.S. 2009/159

118. *Gigi flehmend (Foucaults Lachen),* 2009
Leinwand, Papier, Schmetterling, Ozelot
Canvas, paper, butterfly, ocelot
101 × 50 cm
Andrea Tippel
L.S. 2009/105

119. *Sirenenheime-Buch,* 1999ff
Totalzensierte Pornohefte
Totally censored pornos
29 × 21 cm
Susanne und Dirk Dobke
L.S. 2009/189

120. *Sirenenheime,* 1999ff
Totalzensierte Pornohefte
Totally censored pornos
32 × 42 cm
Stefan Dumfarth
L.S. 2009/86

121. *Sirenenheime,* 1999ff
Totalzensierte Pornohefte
Totally censored pornos
29 × 22 cm
Courtesy Ferenbalm-Gurbrü Station
L.S. 2009/88

122. *Sirenenheime,* 1999ff
Totalzensierte Pornohefte
Totally censored pornos
29 × 22 cm *Courtesy Ferenbalm-Gurbrü Station*
L.S. 2009/91

123. *Sirenenheime-Buch,* 1999ff
Totalzensierte Pornohefte
Totally censored pornos
28 × 21 cm
Private collection, USA
L.S. 2009/90

124. *Sirenenheime,* 1999ff
Totalzensierte Pornohefte
Totally censored pornos
22 × 29 cm
Private collection
L.S. 2009/87

125. *Sirenenheime,* 1999ff
Totalzensierte Pornohefte
Totally censored pornos
29 × 22 cm
Courtesy Ferenbalm-Gurbrü Station
L.S. 2009/82

126. *Sirenenheime,* 1999ff
Totalzensierte Pornohefte
Totally censored pornos
28 × 21 cm
Courtesy Galerie Nikolaus Bischoff
L.S. 2009/84

127. *Sirenenheime,* 1999ff
Totalzensierte Pornohefte
Totally censored pornos
24 × 34 cm
Courtesy Galerie Nikolaus Bischoff
L.S. 2009/78

128. *Sirenenheime,* 1999ff
Totalzensierte Pornohefte
Totally censored pornos
29 × 43 cm
Courtesy Galerie Nikolaus Bischoff
L.S. 2009/85

129. *Sirenenheime,* 1999ff
Totalzensierte Pornohefte
Totally censored pornos
24 × 34 cm
Courtesy Galerie Nikolaus Bischoff
L.S. 2009/80

130. *Sirenenheime,* 1999ff
Totalzensierte Pornohefte
Totally censored pornos
32 × 45 cm
Courtesy Galerie Nikolaus Bischoff
L.S. 2009/79

131. *Sirenenheime,* 1999ff
Totalzensierte Pornohefte
Totally censored pornos
34 × 24 cm
Private collection
L.S. 2009/83

132. *Micronudes,* 2008ff.
Minutie mit Papierausschnitt, Plexiglas
Minutiae with paper cutout, perspex
31 × 24,5 × 5,5 cm

133.–136. *Seltene Paradiesvorstellung I–IV,* 2009
mit / with Helmut Reinisch
Micronudes auf gewebtem Kelim aus Ketschi (Ziegenhaar)
Micronudes on woven kilim made of ketschi (goat hair)
160 × 126, 190 × 129, 140 × 120, 169 × 118 cm
Courtesy Ferenbalm-Gurbrü Station
L.S. 2009/192–195

137. *Schimmelschimmel,* 1999
2116 quadratische Petrischalen, Agar-Agar
2,116 square petri dishes, agar
2 × 345 × 345 cm
L.S. 2009/62

138. *Fibrio Fischerie,* 2003
Leuchtbakterienzucht in verschiedenen Streifen
Plexiglas, Agar-Agar, Bakterien
Luminous bacteria cultures in perspex strips, agar, bacteria
4 × 50 × 50 cm
L.S. 2009/92

139. *Lactowrestling*, 1999
Video and C-print
6 min
Courtesy Galerie Olaf Stüber
L.S. 2009/7

140.–146. *Rhizomorphe Landschaften I-VII*, 2003
C-print
42 × 29,7 cm
L.S. 2009/95

147. *fusarium culmorum*, 2004
Agar-Agar, Schimmelpilz, Glas
Agar, mildew, glass
80 × 50 × 4 cm
Private collection
L.S. 2009/144

148. *botryodiplodia*, 2004
Agar-Agar, Schimmelpilz, Glas
Agar, mildew, glass
80 × 50 × 4 cm
L.S. 2009/145

149. *Tannenbaum weiss meinzman*, 2001
Video
37 min
Courtesy Galerie Olaf Stüber
L.S. 2009/5

150. *Flying Pieces*, 2002
mit / with Peter Stoffel aka blizzers
Video
1:11 min
Courtesy Galerie Olaf Stüber
L.S. 2009/3

151. *Schaumweilen*, 2000
Video
32 min
L.S. 2009/196

152. *Schaumweile I*, 2000
Schaumstoff, Latex
Foam, latex
180 × 180 × 90 cm
L.S. 2009/208

153. *Billy's witch*, 2001
Schaumstoff, Latex, medizinische Pumpe,
Soundsystem, Gleitmittelspringbrunnen
Foam, latex, medical pump, sound system,
lubricant fountain
220 × 140 × 140 cm
Bill Itsch
L.S. 2009/209

154. *Billy's Brunnengesänge*, 2001
mit / with easy-easy foundation
Video and C-print
9 min
Courtesy Galerie Olaf Stüber
L.S. 2009/4

155. *Sirenenheime III*, 2006
Kokospalmwedelflechtwerk, Bambus, Kokosfaser,
innen: Skulptur *Schaumweile V*
Woven coconut palm fronds, bamboo, coconut-fibre,
inside: *Schaumweile V* sculpture
180 × 120 × 240 cm
L.S. 2009/59

156. *Schaumweile V*, 2008
Schaumstoff, Alustab
Foam, aluminium pole
165 × 25 × 60 cm
L.S. 2009/64

157. *Tränen der Sirenen*, 2006
Video and C-print
12 min
Courtesy Galerie Olaf Stüber
L.S. 2009/6

158. *Tabulabor*, 2004
Chemische Destille, verschiedene Materialien
Distillery, mixed media
L.S. 2009/58

159. *Tränen der Sirenen*, 2004
mit / with Anke Wenzel
PE-Folie, Siebdruck, Schnaps,
Polyethylene film, screenprint, schnaps
6 × 10 cm
L.S. 2009/109

160. *Megaron*, 2009
MDF, Latex, Gurken, Schaumstoff auf Leinwand
MDF, latex, cucumber, foam on canvas
180 × 120 × 240 cm
L.S. 2009/61

161. *symphatikus boheme*, 2006
Zwölf Zaunelemente aus Holz, Scharnieren,
Rollen, Acryllack
Twelve wooden fence elements, hinges, wheels,
acrylic paint
Höhe / height 120 cm
L.S. 2009/60

162. *Papa Wata*, 2005
Video
45 min
Courtesy Galerie Olaf Stüber
L.S. 2009/2

163. *Mami Wata*, 2006
Video
12 min
Ben Hübsch
L.S. 2009/1

164. *treeghost*, 2008
Aquarell auf Papier
Watercolour on paper
39 × 30 cm
Private collection, USA
L.S. 2009/141

165. *Stufen der Wandlung*, 2005
mit / with Anke Wenzel
mundgeblasenes Glas
Blown glass
L.S. 2009/106

166. *Palmepiphanie II*, 2006
Aluminium
45 × 3 × 90 cm
L.S. 2009/94

167. *Urkunde I*, 2004
Filzstift auf Papier
Felt pen on paper
25 × 20 cm
L.S. 2009/166

168. *Urkunde II*, 2004
Filzstift auf Papier
Felt pen on paper
18 × 38 cm
L.S. 2009/167

169. *Dugong Mansesse I–IV*, 2004
Fotografie
Photography
84 × 119 cm
L.S. 2009/63

170. *Schaumweile IV*, 2007
Schaumstoff, Alustab
Foam, aluminium pole
165 × 25 × 60 cm
*Margarita und John Belg,
San Juan, Puerto Rico*
L.S. 2009/210

171. *Schaumweile III*, 2006
Schaumstoff, Alustab
Foam, aluminium pole
165 × 25 × 60 cm
Helmut Reivisch
L.S. 2009/211

Impressum / Publishing details

Dieser Katalog erscheint anlässlich der Ausstellung /
This catalogue is published to accompany the exhibition

Dirk Meinzer
Sirenenheime / Siren Homes

Kunsthalle Göppingen
17. Mai – 5. Juli 2009

Ausstellung / Exhibition
Dirk Meinzer, Annett Reckert

Direktor / Director Werner Meyer
Kuratorin / Curator Annett Reckert
Projektassistenz / Project Assistant Lara Eva Sochor
Verwaltung / Administration Jörg Seitz
Kunstvermittlung / Art education programme
Désirée Lempart
FSJ Kultur / Voluntary Social Year in Culture
Katharina Teut

Kunsthalle Göppingen
Marstallstraße 55
73033 Göppingen
Deutschland / Germany
Tel. +49 (0) 7161 650777
Fax +49 (0) 7161 27672

kunsthalle@goeppingen.de
www.kunsthalle-goeppingen.de

© 2009 Dirk Meinzer und die Autoren / and the authors
© VG Bild-Kunst 2009 für die Vergleichsabbildungen /
for the reference material: Jean Dubuffet (p.222),
Max Ernst (p.225)

Herausgeber / Editors
Kunsthalle Göppingen, Annett Reckert
Konzeption und Redaktion / Concept and editing
Annett Reckert, Dirk Meinzer
Texte von / Texts by Tilmann Haffke, Annett Reckert,
Andrea Tippel
Übersetzungen / Translations: Jenny Metcalf,
R. M. Goddard (p. 227–235)
Fotografien und Bildbearbeitung / Photography and image processing Bernd Grether, Frank Kleinbach,
Wolfgang Schuhholz
Gestaltung / Design Bernd Grether
Gesamtherstellung / Production C. Maurer Druckzentrum,
Geislingen an der Steige
Umschlagabbildung / Cover image
Dirk Meinzer, *Dugong Manesse III*, 2004
Buchhandelsausgabe / Trade edition textem verlag, 2009
ISBN 978-3-941613-09-6, www.textem-verlag.de
Museumsausgabe / Museum edition ISBN 978-3-27791-69-5
Auflage / Edition 1000

*Bibliographische Information der Deutschen
Nationalbibliothek* Die Deutsche Nationalbibliothek
verzeichnet diese Publikation in der Deutschen National-
bibliographie; detaillierte bibliographische Daten sind im
Internet über http://dnb.d-nb.de abrufbar.

*Bibliographic information published by the German
National Library* This publication is listed in the German
National Library. Detailed bibliographic data is available
online at http://dnb.d-nb.de.

Printed in Germany

hic Credits

, No. 2, 3, 4, 5, 7, 8, 9, 10, 11, 12,
, 28, 29, 30, 31, 32, 33, 34, 35, 36,
6, 48, 49, 51, 52, 53, 54, 55, 56,
66, 67, 68, 69, 71, 72, 73, 83, 84,
97, 98, 100, 101, 102, 103, 104,
, 111, 112, 113, 116, 117, 118, 119,
, 127, 128, 129, 130, 131, 133, 134,
, 159, 160, 161, 162, 163, 164

, 70, 74, 75, 76, 77, 78, 79, 81,
, 132, 137, 138, 139, 140, 141, 142,
, 151, 152, 153, 154, 155, 157, 165,

7, 18, 20, 23, 24, 27, 43, 45, 47,

Hinweis

Dirk Meinzer verarbeitet in seinen Collagen und Assemblagen Tiere, die dem Washingtoner Artenschutzübereinkommen unterliegen. Die Exemplare stammen aus zollbehördlichen Asservatenkammern. Sie wurden Dirk Meinzer vom Bundesamt für Naturschutz überlassen. Die Exemplare sind gemäß Artikel 51 ff Zollbefreiungsordnung EWG-Nr. 918/83 in Verbindung mit der Durchführungsverordnung EWG 2290/83 abgabenfrei. Der Überlassungsvertrag bezieht sich auf die künstlerische, sowie Ausstellungs-, Lehr- und Unterrichtszwecke. Der vollständige Text des „Übereinkommens über den internationalen Handel mit gefährdeten Arten freilebender Tiere und Pflanzen" – kurz „Washingtoner Artenschutzübereinkommen" – (Convention on International Trade in Endangered Species of Wild Fauna and Flora, CITES) ist im Internet unter www.cites.org nachzulesen.

Note

In his collages and assemblages Dirk Meinzer uses animals that are protected under the Washington Convention. The specimens come from evidence storage facilities of customs authorities. Dirk Meinzer received the specimens from the Federal Agency for Nature Conservation. Pursuant to Article 51 ff of Council Regulation (EEC) No. 918/83 setting up a Community system of reliefs from customs duty, and in conjunction with Implementing Regulation (EEC) No. 2290/83, the specimens are not subject to import duties. The transfer agreement is based on the specimens being used for artistic, exhibition and educational purposes. The full text of the Convention on International Trade in Endangered Species of Wild Fauna and Flora (CITES), also known as the Washington Convention, is available online at www.cites.org.

Dank / Thanks

Für die großzügige Unterstützung der Ausstellung danken wir herzlich allen Leihgeberinnen und Leihgebern. / We would like to thank all lenders for their generous support, without which the exhibition would not have been possible.

Ein besonderer Dank gilt außerdem / Special thanks also go to

Anke Wenzel

und / and

Galerie Nikolaus Bischoff, Christoph Blawert, Margrit Brehm, Bundesamt für Naturschutz (Franz Böhmer), Dirk Dobke, Galerie Ferenbalm-Gurbrü Station, Jan Fischer, Fresnel Optics GmbH, Bianca Gabriel, Bernd Grether, Frank Grether, Tilmann Haffke, Axel Heil, Gamaliel R. Herrera, Corinna Korth, Andreas Krüger, Daniel Kunle, Kunstverein St. Pauli, Tabea Langenkamp, Rolf Luhn, Peter Lynnen, Dirk Martinen, GustavMechlenburg, Hiltrud und Bernd Meinzer, Wenzel Meinzer, Wolfgang Mende, Martin Mende, Toni Mende, Rebekka Posselt, Helmut Reinisch, Svenja Rossa, Marko Schäfer, Wolfgang Schuhholz, Nora Sdun, Lara Eva Sochor, Galerie Olaf Stüber, Andrea Tippel, Fachstelle der Wasser- und Schifffahrtsverwaltung für Verkehrstechniken Koblenz, Edelgard Wenzel

Die Ausstellung Dirk Meinzer. Sirenenheime *in der Kunsthalle Göppingen wurde ermöglicht mit freundlicher Unterstützung der SV Sparkassen Versicherung. / The exhibition* Dirk Meinzer. Siren Homes *was held at the Kunsthalle Göppingen with the generous support of SV Sparkassen Versicherung.*